HAUNTED
MARYLAND

HAUNTED MARYLAND

Dreadful Dwellings, Spine-Chilling Sites, and Terrifying Tales

Darcy Oordt

Globe
Pequot

Guilford, Connecticut

Globe
Pequot

An imprint of Rowman & Littlefield

Distributed by NATIONAL BOOK NETWORK

Copyright © 2016 by Rowman & Littlefield

British Library Cataloguing in Publication Information available

Library of Congress Cataloging-in-Publication Data available

ISBN 978-1-4930-2389-9 (paperback)
ISBN 978-1-4930-2390-5 (ebook)

♾™ The paper used in this publication meets the minimum requirements of American National Standard for Information Sciences—Permanence of Paper for Printed Library Materials, ANSI/NISO Z39.48-1992.

CONTENTS

CONTENTS

ACKNOWLEDGMENTS

First, I have to thank all the people who passed away but never went away. Without them no ghost book could ever be written. I also want to thank my editor, Amy Lyons, and my agent, Regina Ryan. First, they both put up with me, and for that they deserve a medal. But more important, they both have been very supportive and encouraging in this endeavor. So for that, thanks. I'd also like to thank Lauren Szalkiewicz for not running away screaming when I started whining about changes to my "baby."

I also have to thank my father, Darwin Oordt, who has supported me both emotionally and financially when I needed it. Nothing like a dad to be there for you. And thanks to Maggie Moore and Taya Johnston, two friends who constantly tell me that I'm a better writer than I think I am. They may be lying to me, but because they often beat me over the head with hard truths, I like to think not. Also, thank you Perry Corsetti for giving me time off to work on this book.

And finally, thanks to all the jerks who tried to drag me down to their level and pull me off track. At the end of the day, you may have won a battle or two, but in the end you've lost.

INTRODUCTION

When I decided to write a second ghost book, I proposed a book on Baltimore. The editor liked the idea, but asked if I thought I could do the book on the entire state of Maryland. I said sure; in fact it would probably be easier. I was an idiot.

Whenever I start a book, I worry about having enough material. It didn't take me long to realize that wouldn't be possible. Maryland has ghosts everywhere. And they are not here just because a few Civil War battles took place here. It's like people refuse to leave.

While writing this book, I found story after story. And while I wanted to make this book as inclusive as I could, it was impossible to include every story I came across, especially when some of the stories were so interesting.

I've referred to my hometown of Blue Earth, Minnesota, as a ghost desert. There was not one ghost story connected to my town or even the county. Then the oldest building was built in the 1870s. But not all ghosts are from before the 1900s, so I figured it must be because it was a small town. Well, Maryland has shown me how wrong that theory was. Ghosts don't keep to the big cities here. Some of its smaller towns are among the most haunted.

As you read this book, you'll find I rarely mention orbs, psychics, or mediums. This is not an oversight on my part, and it's not that I discount them. The problem I have is that all three are easily faked. While I have encountered spiritual orbs, I also know that they can easily be caused by dust, insects, or countless other items. Everyone has a theory on how to tell "ghostly orbs" from "naturally occurring orbs," but the theories aren't scientific. In my opinion ghost hunters too often make the distinction by saying any orbs taken at a haunted site are ghosts, which isn't true.

I feel the same way about psychics and mediums. While I do believe some people have extrasensory abilities, not all of them are truthful or accurate. Unless what they say is later found to be true, their statements are merely their opinions. While all ghost sightings could be categorized this way, psychics and mediums are frequently paid for their services. They have encouragement to find things, so I don't like to include them in my research.

That's the same reason why I don't include myself in this book, even when I've been to the site. When I go to a haunted site, I already know the stories. That fact could encourage me to think every experience is caused by the paranormal. "My phone died. It must be the ghosts!" (Or it could be that you were chatting on Facebook for an hour before you arrived and you didn't fully charge it the night before . . .)

I am, however, a believing skeptic when it comes to ghosts. That means I believe in ghosts. I have had experiences with ghosts. But that doesn't mean I believe that everything people say are ghosts truly are ghosts. A true paranormal experience should be one of exclusion. Every other possible explanation should be excluded before claiming it was a ghost.

Once upon a time, paranormal reality programs believed and followed this practice. But disproving ghosts doesn't get you ratings. So they stopped looking too hard to find what might actually be causing a place to be "haunted." And part of me doesn't blame them. Most of the sites they go to want to be haunted. Telling them it's nothing is like telling a child there's no Santa Claus (which we all know is a lie— Santa is real!).

Part 1

BALTIMORE

Baltimore is the largest city in Maryland and the second-largest seaport in the mid-Atlantic. The city was founded in 1729 and is named after the first proprietary governor of the Province of Maryland, Lord Baltimore. Baltimore has more ghost stories than those created by Edgar Allan Poe, who lived, died, and is buried in Baltimore. All ghost enthusiasts need to put Fell's Point on their bucket list, as it is one of the most haunted neighborhoods in the country. Baltimore also has several haunted ships and Fort McHenry, which defended the city during the War of 1812 and inspired Francis Scott Key to write "The Star-Spangled Banner."

Chapter 1
Edgar Allan Poe

Edgar Allan Poe is one of Baltimore's most famous residents. During his life Poe frequently moved and lived in a variety of cities, including Baltimore. However, he died in Baltimore on October 7, 1849, and Baltimore is where he is buried. This has created a permanent link between the city and the master of macabre. It's only fitting that several locations connected with Poe are haunted, although not always by Poe.

Edgar Allan Poe may be known as the Master of the Macabre, but horror comprised a small portion of his writing legacy. He is also credited with inventing the detective story and helping develop the literary genres of science fiction and mystery.

During his troubled life Poe lived in a variety of cities including New York, Philadelphia, Richmond, Boston, and Baltimore. All the cities have claimed a portion of Poe's legacy, but none more so than Baltimore, which even named their football team the Ravens after one of Poe's poems. But Poe didn't just live in Baltimore, he died there.

On September 28, 1849, Poe arrived in Baltimore. It was supposed to be a stop on his way to Philadelphia. Yet several days later he was still there. On October 3, 1849, Joseph W. Walker sent a note to Dr. J. E. Snodgrass about "a gentleman . . . who goes under the cognomen of Edgar A. Poe, and who appears in great distress, & he says he is acquainted with you, and I assure you, he is in need of immediate assistance." Snodgrass arrived with Poe's uncle, Henry Herring, and arranged for him to be transported to Washington College Hospital. Poe died on October 7, 1849.

What happened to Poe after he arrived in Baltimore has never been definitively proven. What is known is that when he was found, Poe was no longer wearing his own clothes, but was dressed in dirty and tattered clothing that didn't fit him. A number of theories on where Poe went between September 28 and October 3 and what caused his death exist—too many to even list here. Cause of death theories include hypoglycemia, murder, suicide, alcoholism, cholera, diabetes, apoplexy, brain disease, brain tumor, syphilis, enzyme deficiency, epilepsy, delirium tremens, and meningeal inflammation.

Poe himself could not have written a more mysterious end for himself had he been given the chance, which seems a fitting legacy for the great writer. Shortly after Poe's death, his literary rival, Rufus Griswold, wrote a libelous obituary about Poe. It seems Griswold was upset over some things Poe wrote about him, and he decided to get his revenge. He followed the obituary with a memoir that portrayed Poe as a womanizing, insane drunk who lacked morals and friends.

Ironically, Griswold hoped to get the public to dismiss Poe's works. His attack had the opposite effect and increased the sale of Poe's works. Griswold's image of Poe stuck, even though Griswold himself faded into obscurity.

EDGAR ALLAN POE HOUSE
203 NORTH AMITY STREET, BALTIMORE, 21223

The Edgar Allan Poe House and Museum is a brick row house built around 1830. Edgar Allan Poe lived in the house from

1832 until 1835 with his paternal grandmother; his aunt, Maria Clemm; and her two children, Virginia and Henry. He had just been discharged from the US Military Academy at West Point. Shortly after leaving the house, Poe married his cousin Virginia when she was thirteen and he was twenty-seven.

In 1941 the city of Baltimore planned to demolish the house, but it was saved by the Edgar Allan Poe Society. After doing extensive repairs, the society opened the house to the public in 1949. In 1977 the City of Baltimore's Commission for Historical and Architectural Preservation elected Jeff Jerome as curator of the museum. On September 26, 2012, the house was transferred to a new organization created to manage the house, Poe Baltimore. The change in management meant that after thirty-four years, Jerome would no longer be the curator of the house. Poe Baltimore did extensive renovations on the house before reopening it on October 5, 2013.

Most of the tales of the hauntings at the Poe House come from the period when Jerome was curator. Early on a friend talked him into holding a séance in the house that would be broadcast live over the radio on Halloween night 1979. The house had recently opened after renovations, so it was believed the séance would be good publicity. At 11:45 p.m. several of the people attending the séance looked toward the stairway leading toward Poe's bedroom, but no one said anything. After the séance was over, one of them approached Jerome and told him that his friend upstairs could come down as he hadn't fooled them. Jerome asked what they were talking about.

The attendees—who included a psychic, two policemen, and two radio technicians—had all heard heavy footsteps walking around on the floor above them. They believed it was a stunt. Jerome assured them that no one was upstairs.

A large, heavyset woman has been seen on the third floor of the house. She is described as middle-aged and formally dressed. People like to speculate that this is Poe's grandmother. But it could be any number of women who lived in the house after Poe left it.

David Keltz was giving a tour in the house when he felt someone rap him hard on his back. He turned around to see who was behaving so rudely, but no one was behind him. Another night, Keltz was doing a reading of Poe's work on the second floor when the ghost decided to put on its own performance. One by one his audience turned around as if they were poked in the back. It was like the ghost was working down the line.

An actress was on the second floor preparing for a dramatic reading of "Berenice" when she suddenly screamed. Jerome raced to the room and discovered the woman, half-dressed, in hysterics. She told Jerome that as she was getting ready, the window began to tilt in its pane. Then it flew out of the pane and crashed in the center of the room. The actress was so distressed, the performance was canceled. Later Jerome tried to re-create the event, but couldn't.

Windows and doors in the Poe House have been known to open and close on their own. People have reported seeing lights moving through the house when it is unoccupied. Others report hearing a mysterious muttering.

A few have even claimed to have seen Poe's ghost. Jerome usually discounts these stories, as they usually describe Poe with a mustache. When Poe lived in the house, he didn't have one.

THE HORSE YOU CAME IN ON SALOON
1626 Thames Street, Baltimore, 21231

The Horse You Came In On Saloon is believed to be the oldest bar in Baltimore and claims to be the last drinking spot of Edgar Allan Poe. Poe was found lying in a gutter outside a polling place, Gunner's Hall, which was located near the corner of East Lombard and High Streets. While The Horse was a drinking establishment at the time, no evidence that Poe visited the bar exists.

That doesn't prevent people from referring to the ghost here as "Edgar." Several psychics who visited the bar agreed it is the spirit of Edgar Allan Poe that haunts the establishment. And it would seem the ghost agrees. On one occasion a bartender made several negative remarks about Poe. Suddenly several barstools flew across the bar and slammed into the wall. Realizing her mistake, she immediately poured a shot and left it at the end of the bar as a peace offering.

Since then it is commonplace for bartenders to pour the ghost a shot whenever they get scared. Some say when they return the following morning, the glass is found cleaned and put away. Others say the shot has yet to be touched.

Another bartender was opening the bar for the evening. She walked by one of the cash registers, when it suddenly opened. She closed it, but before she got too far, it opened again. This happened three more times. She later told her story to another bartender, who reported the same thing had happened to him several times.

Other paranormal events in the bar include a safe door that slams itself shut, chandeliers that swing aggressively, and strange whispering being heard. Numerous white orbs of light have also been witnessed by employees and guests at the bar.

WESTMINSTER HALL
519 WEST FAYETTE STREET, BALTIMORE, 21201

The Westminster Burying Grounds was established in 1786. The church was built later, in 1852, above a number of graves. This created catacombs underneath the church. The hope was that having a church on the property would protect the cemetery from being disturbed.

In the eighteenth century, grave robbing was a terrible problem. As soon as someone was buried, someone else would come along and dig the body up. The bodies were sold to medical schools for anatomical dissection. But body snatching was only one of the problems Westminster faced.

A lot of strange occurrences in the cemetery were reported in an April 1966 newspaper article written by Joel Shurkin. In March of that year, a reporter discovered smoke coming from one of the crypts. He opened it up and discovered a homeless man camping out with a fire. Evidence showed that this was not the first time it had happened.

Shurkin also reported about some earlier issues at the church and cemetery. In 1929, when Dr. Bruce McDonald became pastor of the church, he found quite a sight. McDonald said, "I found all the tombs in the graveyard open and children running about the street with skulls on broomsticks."

Several men committed suicide from the top of the church steeple by winding the bell rope around their necks and jumping. This announced their suicide with an eerie bell ringing. On another occasion a crypt was opened for a burial only to discover that it was already occupied. A victim had been shoved into the crypt alive and the door sealed from the outside. Apparently someone wanted to commit murder ala "The Cask of Amontillado."

Although there are a number of graves at Westminster, the most famous has to be that of Edgar Allan Poe.

After Poe's death he was buried near the back of the cemetery near his grandfather. His cousin, Neilson Poe, paid for a marble headstone for him, but it was destroyed after a train derailed and plowed through the monument yard where it was being kept. For a number of years, the only thing that marked Poe's grave was a sandstone block labeled "No. 80."

Then Paul Hamilton Hayne wrote a newspaper article about the sad condition of Poe's grave. A Baltimore schoolteacher, Sara Sigourney Rice, decided to help raise funds for a new monument. In 1875 a new monument was erected. According to newspapers printed at the time, Poe's body was excavated in October 6, 1875, so the foundation for the new monument could be poured. But the scheduled unveiling of the monument was delayed when it was decided a more prominent position for Poe's grave was required. Eventually he was moved to the front portion of the cemetery.

Although Poe's ghost has never been seen at his grave, another almost ghostly visitor has: the legendary Poe Toaster. The Poe Toaster is an unknown man who appeared at Poe's grave in the early morning hours on January 19 (Poe's birthday). He would place three red roses and a half-full bottle of cognac. It is unknown exactly when the Toaster began his ritual, but some say he was first sighted in the 1930s.

Jeff Jerome, curator at the Edgar Allan Poe House and Museum, witnessed the event from the safety of the church for several decades starting in 1976. According to Jerome, the man usually wore a black hat and coat with a white scarf that concealed his face. He would raise a glass of cognac in a silent toast and then take a sip. He then put the roses and bottle of cognac at the base of the grave. Then he put his hand on the top of the tombstone and put his head down. After five minutes he would leave.

Jerome first told his story to newspaper reporters in the 1980s. *Life* magazine picked up on the story and published a grainy picture of the mysterious Toaster in 1990. After that, interest in the Toaster grew, as did the audiences around Poe's grave on January 19.

Then, in 2007, Sam Porpora stepped forward and claimed he had made up the story in the 1960s to generate interest in the church. Jerome disputes Porpora's claim, saying that newspaper articles that date back to the 1950s mention the Toaster.

The last sighting of the Poe Toaster was in 2009, on the two-hundredth anniversary of Poe's birth. Why he stopped is unclear. Some believe it was the large crowds that had started gathering, while others feel that he decided to stop at the two-hundred-year anniversary.

In 2008 Porpora claimed Poe's body had been snatched after burial and sold to the University of Maryland School of Medicine. While body snatching was a huge problem at the time of Poe's death, no evidence exists that his body was stolen. When his body was exhumed and moved in 1875, newspapers reported seeing a decaying body in the coffin with Poe's features.

There are a few ghosts associated with the cemetery. Visitors have heard children playing. Others have spotted a man wearing a gray vest in the catacomb areas. Perhaps now that the Poe Toaster is gone, other spirits at Westminster will step up and become active.

Chapter 2
Fell's Point

Fell's Point sits on a mere seventy-five acres, but it has to be the most haunted area of Baltimore. Usually a place this haunted has a major tragedy connected to it, but not in this case. It seems people like being here so much, they return in the afterlife. Although some businesses may wish they didn't, like the one that requires employees to sign a waiver exempting them from any damages the ghost might inflict on them. But don't worry; the other ghosts at Fell's Point are friendlier.

Fell's Point (sometimes spelled "Fells Point") originally belonged to William Fell. He built a house there and named it "Fell's Prospect." After he died in 1746, his son Edward took control of the property. He established the town of Fell's Point in 1763. Fell's Point was incorporated into Baltimore in 1773.

Some of the US Navy's first ships were built at Fell's Point, including the USS *Constellation*. The area was more famous for producing Baltimore clippers—topsail schooners known for their speed and handling. Between 1784 and 1821, around eight hundred ships were built at Fell's Point. Among them was the original *Pride of Baltimore,* built by Thomas Kemp during the War of 1812, and the *Constellation* in 1797.

Frederick Douglass was hired out to a Fell's Point shipbuilder in 1835. He taught himself how to read and write here. The area remained in the shipbuilding trade until the

Civil War, when it could no longer handle the larger ships being built. Canning companies and other industries quickly replaced the shipyards.

In the 1800s, Fell's Point was a rough area. A map of Fell's Point published in 1888 listed 323 saloons and 113 brothels. Crime, drunkenness, and other immoral acts were the norm here. But that didn't stop sailors and immigrants from making it their home. At the turn of the nineteenth century, around 31,500 people lived in Fell's Point.

Fell's Point managed to avoid being destroyed by the Baltimore Fire of 1904. But it was almost destroyed in 1965 when federal transit planners proposed to link Interstate 83 and Interstate 95. Local residents quickly rallied together to prevent the destruction, and Fell's Point was added to the National Register of Historic Places. In the 1990s Fell's Point achieved fame as the setting for the NBC drama *Homicide: Life on the Street.*

Today Fell's Point is a middle-class neighborhood with a thriving nightlife and plenty of ghosts.

THE ADMIRAL FELL INN
888 South Broadway, Baltimore, 21231

Trip Advisor has named the Admiral Fell Inn as one of America's Top Ten Haunted Hotels. And once you hear the stories, it's easy to see why. Over half a dozen ghosts have been documented in the hotel.

In a video posted on YouTube, manager John Lowe told of his own experience at the hotel. According to Lowe, "I was giving a tour at the hotel to a guest and we're walking down the halls when we saw sitting on the steps this old man and this little girl. As we got closer the old man disappeared and the little girl ran down the hall and then she too disappeared."

Lowe also told about a housekeeper who refused to work in room 413. According to Lowe she told him, "Every time I clean the room I feel breezes, somebody brushing by me, touching my arms, touching my shoulders. I just get scared. I can't do it anymore." Rumor says a man died in that room, but nothing has been proven.

A guest staying in room 218 was awoken in the middle of the night by the sound of the floorboards creaking. He opened his eyes and saw the ghost of a nurse in his room. She vanished through the wall. Her ghost may remain from when the building was run by the Port Mission Women's Auxiliary. The auxiliary opened a boardinghouse in the 1900s called The Anchorage. It was designed to be a safe harbor with Christian values where sailors could stay. Eventually it was taken over by the YMCA, which ran it until 1955.

Another guest was in her bed attempting to sleep when she felt someone sit at the end of her bed. She opened her eyes and saw an orb. She sat up to get a better look, and the orb disappeared. Another guest awoke to find a little boy standing in the doorway of his room. As soon as he made eye contact with the ghost, the doors of his room swung open, and the boy disappeared.

Hotel staff has given names to two of the nosiest ghosts in the hotel. Bitsy is the ghost who disrupts the second floor, while Grady likes to make a ruckus on the third floor. They are known for making loud thumping noises. Thankfully they quiet down the minute any of the guests call the front desk to complain.

The hotel closed during Hurricane Isabel in 2003. A few managers were assigned to stay and look after the hotel. Iowna Diaz, assistant hotel manager, was alone in the lobby when she heard footsteps and music on the floor above her. It sounded as if a party was going on. As soon as another manager joined her, the noises stopped. The following night, John Lowe heard the same sounds. The footsteps kept growing louder and louder until the ceiling started shaking. Again, as soon as he was joined by another manager, the noise stopped. Apparently the ghosts took advantage of the empty hotel to throw a party.

Today the hotel management truly embraces its ghosts and offers ghost tours of the hotel that include hired actors to give first-person narratives of the stories. They also have daily "ghost" teas and other ghostly events.

BERTHA'S MUSSELS
734 SOUTH BROADWAY, BALTIMORE, 21231

Bertha's Restaurant, also known as Bertha's Mussels, requires new employees to sign a waiver that prevents them from holding the owners accountable for any emotional distress they might suffer at the hands of the ghost. They are also told never to enter the storeroom alone.

One employee who disregarded the warning quickly regretted it. He entered the room and discovered that instead of a storeroom, it had transformed into a bedroom. Sunlight poured from the windows, even though it was night. As he looked around the room, he saw a little girl playing in the corner. When the girl turned toward him, he was horrified to find she had no face. He tore down the stairs and out of the restaurant in a panic. Another waiter also encountered a young girl in the storeroom. However his encounter was not so creepy. According to him, the girl appeared startled by his appearance and quickly faded away.

But that's just one of the ghosts here. Another disturbing ghost called "the Lady in the Gray Cloak" follows patrons up the stairs before disappearing. What's so creepy about that? The woman is described as being nothing but a skeleton with two eyeballs and a very nice gray cloak. One patron may have encountered the Lady in the Gray Cloak in the bathroom. While she was taking care of business, she heard a woman ask her, "How long will you be in there?" When she came out, no one else was in the bathroom, nor had anyone been seen going into the bathroom. Since the bathroom is close to where the Lady in the Gray Cloak is seen, they figured it must have been her.

In an upstairs apartment, the tenant's cat would freeze with its hair raised on its back. The cat would remain frozen for long moments. On the same floor in a dance studio, an employee saw a woman in black wearing a large hat in the mirror. A man was coming down the stairs when he saw someone behind him. He turned and saw a man wearing a large hat and a dark cloak standing on the stairs.

The man on the stairs may be the same man another employee saw. At 3:30 one morning, an employee working in an adjoining building saw a dark figure on the security monitor. She described him as a large figure, very tall, and he was walking through the downstairs bar. She thought it odd that an employee would be in the building at that hour, but the security alarms had not gone off to indicate an intruder. Finally she decided to go downstairs and peer into the window of the bar, but she didn't see anything. So she went back upstairs to finish her work. Three more times she saw the figure appear on the screen.

A young girl has been seen on the second floor. She has been heard skipping in a corner, causing a rhythmic sound. Workers in the building early in the morning have reported hearing footsteps on the floor above them, even though no one else is in the building.

Although Bertha's Restaurant has been around only a few decades, the building that houses it dates back to the late 1700s or early 1800s. Like all older buildings in Baltimore, it has been transformed a number of times and has seen all sorts of tragedies. It's not surprising that a few of the people who lived and worked here ended up staying.

DUDA'S TAVERN
1600 THAMES STREET, BALTIMORE, 21231

Duda's Tavern has a unique ghost story connected to it involving a former regular named Doc. Back in Doc's day, Duda's had a jukebox, and one of the selections was a polka. Doc loved the song and was known for playing it frequently throughout the night. No matter how much people would complain, Doc continued to play it.

When Doc passed away, the owners of the bar had him cremated. Since they had never heard Doc mention a family, they planned to scatter his ashes in the Chesapeake Bay where he liked to fish. Before they could, they were approached by the girlfriend of one of their beer distributors. She asked them if they had someone's remains.

Astonished, they admitted they did. She told them that she was a psychic and they needed to hold onto those ashes a little bit longer.

A few days later, Doc's brother arrived in town. He had heard that his brother had died and wanted to take his ashes home to bury in the family plot. But Doc wasn't finished. Shortly after his brother left, the jukebox suddenly started playing his favorite polka. But no one had programmed the jukebox, and the record containing the polka had been removed from the jukebox after Doc had died.

Doc's ghost was seen by an electrician working in the building. He freaked out and left after Doc disappeared before his eyes. People also report hearing footsteps and discovering chairs moved around when no one else is in the building.

LEADBETTER'S TAVERN
1639 Thames Street, Baltimore, 21231

Leadbetter's Tavern was opened in the 1960s and named after blues singer Huddie "Lead Belly" Ledbetter. While some claim his spirit was captured in a photograph taken at the tavern, other ghosts are much more active here.

The first ghost is of a sailor. He is seen late at night wandering around the tavern, walking straight through walls. He doesn't seem to notice anyone or anything around him. Some speculate that he was a sailor whose body was dumped behind the building in the 1800s. "Shanghaiing" was popular in Fell's Point until the 1950s. It involved kidnapping an able-bodied man and forcing him into service on a ship.

It's possible someone attempted to shanghai the young man, got too forceful, and killed him. Then, when Leadbetter's expanded, they enclosed the area behind the building where the man was killed. Rumor says the expansion uncovered a body with a shattered skull in the back alley, but no record of this event was found.

The second ghost at Leadbetter's is of a man who lived on the second floor of the building in the 1970s. The man was abusive toward his wife and son. Eventually the son had had enough and shot the man. A bartender who lived in the apartment after the event once had a friend who had had too much to drink sleep it off on his couch. Suddenly, the door flew open and a huge, angry-looking man entered the room and screamed at her to leave. She quickly complied.

The man's son actually returned to the bar in an attempt to communicate with his father. But rather than settle the spirit, it made the haunting worse. The manager was advised by a practicing witch to set out a bowl of candy as a bribe to the ghost. She claimed that Brach's peppermints are a favorite of ghosts. Having nothing to lose, the manager did just that. He placed the bowl in a spot where human guests would be unable to either see or access it easily. A few days later he noticed one of the mints had turned pink, as if someone had licked it, except the candy was still in the wrapper. The candies also started disappearing one by one.

Another ghost is of a man with long brown hair and tattered clothing. He appears in the ladies' room mirror. Women using the facility report seeing him standing behind them. Sometimes he even appears to be reaching out to touch their hair. But when they spin around to confront him, he's gone.

Leadbetter's was sold in 2014 and rumored to be closing. However, the bar remained open, although the name has changed to Leadbetter's II Tavern.

WHISTLING OYSTER
807 South Broadway, Baltimore, 21231

According to Read Hopkins, who purchased the Whistling Oyster in 1973, he and another bartender were closing one night when the bartender claimed to see a woman pacing behind the bar. He said she was wearing a colonial dress with a white cap and apron. Patrons who have seen her often approach her thinking she's simply in costume; but when they ask her for a drink, she vanishes.

Hopkins's wife once saw a man dressed in colonial-era clothing sweeping the floor near the fireplace. He has been described as being a middle-age black man wearing a leather apron and red-and-white checkered shirt. This ghost doesn't seem to notice anyone else in the bar, which may explain why he keeps moving the ash bucket.

One night bartender Warren Newcomb found the bucket in the aisle between two tables. Fearing someone would trip over it, he moved it next to the fireplace. Ten minutes later, someone pointed out to him that the ash bucket had been moved so it was in the aisle again. But no one had been back in that part of the building. After this happened several more times, no one wanted to move the ash can, so it was allowed to stay there. The Whistling Oyster closed in 2011. A cocktail bar, Rye, is currently in its place.

ELSEWHERE AROUND FELL'S POINT
ADMIRAL'S CUP

The Admiral's Cup is haunted by its former owner, Helen Bochenski. She sold the property in the early 1980s, but continued to live in an apartment in the building until her death. Since it was shortly thereafter that the ghost appeared, everyone figured it must be Helen.

A bartender saw a young woman pass through the bar and disappear up the staircase. On another occasion, manager Jeff Stone was closing up. He turned off all the lights and televisions, but one of the TVs refused to remain turned off. Finally, he gave up and told Helen she could watch all the TV she wanted. He left it on, set the alarm, and left for the night. Admiral's Cup is located at 1647 Thames Street.

CAT'S EYE PUB

The Cat's Eye Pub has a "Wall of Death" with photos of customers and employees who have died, and at least two of the people featured on the wall seem to have returned to watch over the bar. They are a former owner, Kenny Oyre, and a bartender, Jeff Knapp. These two men were pranksters while they were alive and continue to cause havoc during their afterlife. Model ships and pictures have been known to fly off the shelves and across the room. When visiting, it would be wise not to speak ill of the dead. A bartender was talking trash about Kenny when the photograph of Kenny fell off the wall and struck her in the head.

During a renovation of the pub, workers found several red light switches on the walls, like those commonly found in brothels. When a prostitute was not occupied with a customer, she'd flip her switch and turn on a red lightbulb that indicated she was available. The workers covered up the area with drywall, but employees and patrons still claim to hear the switches make loud clicking noises as if they are being turned on and off. Cat's Eye Pub is located at 1730 Thames Street.

FELL FAMILY CEMETERY

A well-dressed man wearing eighteenth-century clothing is seen standing in the middle of Shakespeare Street. He stands there a moment before walking toward the small cemetery located on the street and vanishing. Other times he is seen walking westward down the street away from Broadway. The ghost is believed to be one of the four Fell family members buried under the tombstone there.

Point founder, William, and his brother Edward are both said to be buried there, along with William's son Edward and grandson William. There was an old graveyard there where several people were buried. However, as Quakers, the Fells were more likely to have been buried in the graveyard at the Quaker meetinghouse on Fayette Street.

Some speculate the ghost is the older William Fell, upset that his family homestead was transformed into a city. Or the ghost could be his grandson William, who died under mysterious circumstances. The cemetery is sometimes referred to as the "Fell-Bond Cemetery," because the location was once known as the Bond Cemetery. The Fell Family Cemetery is located on Shakespeare Street between 1603 and 1609.

Friends at Fell's Point

This building was once a motel and rumored to have been a brothel. The ghost of a woman has been heard walking the second floor. People have also smelled her perfume in the building. One man claimed he felt as if someone was trying to strangle him while he was on the second floor.

On the first floor, a bartender claims that a man sitting at the bar vanished in front of his eyes. Others have seen an old lady in a rocking chair in the billiards room. Others have reported feeling cold spots and seeing shadowy figures throughout the building. Friends at Fell's Point was located at 1634 Aliceanna Street. It is now known as Sticky Rice, an Asian fusion restaurant.

Max's Taphouse

Max's Taphouse is actually three buildings combined into one. The buildings date back to the 1800s and have housed restaurants, boardinghouses, and brothels over the years. At one point it was even a chicken slaughterhouse, which explains why employees have run out of the basement claiming to have seen decapitated chickens running around.

A woman in white has been seen on the second floor, and a cook once felt a hand slide from his head to his neck here. On the first floor, bottles have been seen floating through the air. A male figure was also seen disappearing through a wall.

On the third floor, a window refuses to stay shut even after it was nailed that way. Staff have also heard footsteps walking around the floor. One time they called the police, fearing an intruder was in the building. The police brought dogs in the building, but the dogs refused to venture onto the third floor. Max's Taphouse is located on 737 South Broadway.

ROBERT LONG HOUSE

Dating back to the 1760s, the Robert Long House is the oldest urban house in Baltimore, which pretty much requires it to be haunted. The house was set to be torn down in 1969, but the Society for the Preservation of Federal Hill and Fell's Point saved it and restored it. Their office is located on the second floor of the building.

People report "weird feelings" on the first floor, which has been restored so it appears similar to when Robert Long lived there. Noises are heard from the second floor. The third floor, which was added in the latter half of the 1800s, is a cold and uncomfortable place to be, although no one knows why. The Robert Long House is located at 812 South Ann Street.

WHARF RAT

In July 1907 John Rutkowski was sitting in his bar, Buck Gardeners, listening to his gramophone. He found particular enjoyment in a brass band rendition of "The Star-Spangled Banner." After playing it a number of times, one of his patrons demanded he turn it off. John refused and told the man if he didn't like it, he could leave. The patron grew angry, got up, and smashed the record into pieces. John immediately threw the man out of his bar.

A short time later, the man returned to the bar with his brother and a gun. He shot John dead. The man and his brother stood trial for murder. But the shooter was only convicted of manslaughter and received three years. His brother was found not guilty.

Perhaps it was the lack of justice that caused John's ghost to remain in his former bar, now known as the Wharf Rat. His ghost is frequently seen in the second story windows and near the twelve-foot fireplace. A former cook claims to have seen his ghost appear beside her every night while she was doing prep work. He never spoke, but only looked at her mournfully before disappearing. Wharf Rat is located at 801 South Ann Street.

WATERFRONT HOTEL

Fans of *Homicide: Life on the Street* may recognize the Waterfront Hotel as the bar owned by detectives in the series. Today it is known as the Waterfront Hotel, but it is a restaurant and bar. The building was built in 1771 and still has a lot of the original features.

People have reported hearing footsteps, voices, and children laughing on the upper floors. On a particular occasion a patron reported seeing a child run out of the fireplace and across the room before it disappeared. Bar stools have reportedly moved around when no one was in the room. Rumors say that someone died in the building in the 1970s, but nothing has been proven. The Waterfront Hotel is located at 1710 Thames Street.

Chapter 3

Historic Ships

Located in the Inner Harbor of Baltimore, the Historic Ships in Baltimore is a maritime museum with four ships and a lighthouse. Entrance into the museum allows you access to all of them. Since three of the ships on permanent exhibit are haunted by men who died while serving on-board, that's a good deal.

Another ship, the Pride of Baltimore II, *is located down the river on Lighthouse Point. It is actually a reproduction of the* Pride *of Baltimore. It goes out for day cruises and serves as a good will ambassador for the city. It is also said to be haunted by its former crew.*

USS *CONSTELLATION*
301 East Pratt Street, Baltimore, 21202

The first USS *Constellation* was built in Fell's Point and launched in 1797. She carried 38 guns and 350 men. She served the US Navy well until she was decommissioned and broken up in 1853. The following year another USS *Constellation* was launched. Although her dimensions were similar, she carried only 22 guns and 240 men. She was used in the Navy until 1933. She is the last Civil War–era naval vessel and sail-powered warship built by the US Navy.

For most of the twentieth century, historians believed there was only one USS *Constellation,* which was modified in 1853. This idea was promoted by the city of Baltimore, which rebuilt sections of the ship to resemble the 1797 ship. It wasn't until 1991 that researchers concluded the current ship had been built in 1853. However, the new ship used some of the original timbers for the 1797 ship, which explained the confusion. This could explain why ghosts from the original ship may be haunting the newer one.

The USS *Constellation* has a long history of hauntings. One of the earliest accounts of a ghost on the ship was recorded by Moses Safford in his diary. Safford kept a diary from March 1862 until February 1865 while serving on the ship. One interesting passage was recorded on June 21, 1863, about a crewman named Ike Simmons who had been given five days in the brig in double irons for singing while in the brig. Simmons wrote, "According to [Ike], Nichols, the Negro, and Raynes, the Kanaka, who died recently on the ship, appeared before him and danced in the brig outside of his cell and he sang to them."

While Ike could have made up that story, Safford added something that suggests otherwise. "The ship's corporal told me as something which was puzzling him that this morning he was found in the brig five buckets stacked up in a peculiar way and which had stood up in spite of the motion of the ship. Simmons was in a cell and could not have stacked them and the corporal had the only key to the door of the brig which was locked."

Safford goes on to add, "I am informed the mysterious occurrences or manifestations have annoyed and tested the nerves of men who have been confined to the brig before. Some of these incidents have been mentioned only to the Master-at-Arms. Twice on stormy nights last fall Campbell, the captain of the forecastle, whom we list in the Atlantic was supposed to have been seen standing near the lee cat-head."

Safford also wrote, "Whatever may be the explanation of these phenomena the sentence which Simmons has received will tend to discourage the men from giving undue publicity to their supernatural observations." It seems that great pains were taken to keep the ship's ghosts a secret.

In the 1950s, the USS *Pike* was moored next to the *Constellation* for use as a naval reserve training ship. Sailors on the *Pike* reported hearing strange noises and seeing unidentified shapes and lights moving along the decks. Lieutenant Commander Allen R. Brougham decided in 1955 to investigate and spent the night on the ship with a photographer.

According to Brougham, shortly before midnight he detected a faint smell of gunpowder right before the spirit manifested itself. He described the ghost as "a phosphorescently glowing, translucent ectoplasmic manifestation of a late Eighteenth Century sailor complete with gold striped trouser, cocked hat and sword." He was able to snap a photograph of the ghost before it disappeared. The photograph was later published in the *Baltimore Sun*. Many believe this to show Captain Thomas Truxton, the first captain of the 1797 *Constellation*. Others have seen Truxton on the forecastle deck above the first full deck.

Truxton may also be the ghost who appeared to a priest in 1964. As the priest was leaving the ship, he stopped to praise employees for the marvelous tour he had been given by a man dressed in an 1812 Navy uniform. The employees were puzzled because they had no guides dressed in costume and had not seen anyone matching that description. They searched the ship, but it was empty.

Truxton may be joined by a ghost of his own making. Neil Harvey's full-bodied apparition has been seen moving along the decks of the ship. Harvey served on the first *Constellation* under Truxton. In 1799 he was sentenced to death. The circumstances of his death are somewhat in dispute. One version says that he had run from his post during the ship's battle with the French frigate *L'Insurgente*. Captain Truxton ordered another sailor to stab Harvey with his sword before tying him to a cannon and firing.

Another version of Harvey's story says that he fell asleep while on duty after the battle. He was so overcome with shame, that he smuggled a gun into the brig and shot himself. Harvey's ghost appears real, and he is often mistaken for a reenactor.

Another former sailor haunts the gun and forecastle decks. He is described as looking mournful. He is believed to be the ghost of a sailor who hanged himself to escape the conditions on the ship. Still another one appears to be running for his life along one of the decks. Some simply report hearing and feeling people running along the deck. There is also a young boy about eleven who has been seen on the ship. Psychic Sybil Leek claims the boy had been stabbed to death by two crewmen in the 1820s.

But not all the ghosts are from when the ship was in active service. Carl Hansen was a security guard on the ship until 1963 or 1965. He was fired after being replaced by a modern security system. After he passed away, his ghost started appearing aboard the ship. He was seen sitting next to a young girl during a Halloween party. Others report seeing his ghost playing cards on a lower deck. Some even say the priest in 1964 described Hansen and not Truxton.

In 1976 employee James Hudgins told a reporter, "One time, I switched on the alarm system, turned off all the lights and locked up for the night. The next day, the place was still locked from the inside, but the lights and a radio were on." On another occasion repairmen reported hearing moans and cries coming from the lower decks. Investigations showed no one else on the ship.

USCGC *TANEY*

The USCGC *Taney* is a US Coast Guard High Endurance Cutter commissioned in 1936. In 1937 it searched for Amelia Earhart after her disappearance on July 2. The *Taney* has the distinction of being the last ship afloat that fought at Pearl Harbor on December 7, 1941, although she wasn't moored in Pearl Harbor during the attack.

She went on to serve as a command ship during the Battle of Okinawa in 1945. During the battle she shot down five enemy planes during 119 separate engagements. She also served during the Korean and Vietnam Wars. Forty-five years after Pearl Harbor, she was decommissioned and turned over to the city of Baltimore for use as a museum ship.

In a 2014 press release, Sarah Rauscher, Historic Ships in Baltimore's education coordinator, related some of the ghost stories associated with the ship. She says most of the activity occurs near the Chief's Mess and damage control office, which are at the front of the ship.

"Overnight workers doing rounds will walk by the Chief's Mess and see someone inside the room, which isn't possible because all of the rooms on display like this are under lock and key," Rauscher said.

She also said people see ghostly forms moving along the decks and past open hatchways or hear someone moving frantically through the ship, but no one is seen. Another time, a parent supervising during an overnight youth program saw a person standing in the passageway near the damage control office. But when he checked, no one was there.

Ghostly footsteps have also been heard walking through the ship. People have also heard voices, including one that seemed to be speaking Japanese near the galley. This may be a pilot who was rumored to have been brought on the ship for medical attention during the Battle of Okinawa. He supposedly died while on the ship, but no record of him being brought onboard exists.

Others report hearing the sound of the ship's engines running when they are not on. But perhaps the most unexplained is the sound of commands that come through the public address system. The system no longer works.

The Atlantic Paranormal Society (TAPS) investigated the ship during season 8 of *Ghost Hunters,* which aired in 2012. During the episode, Patrick Aquia, a logistics coordinator, reported that people see figures walk by the portholes and that lights turn off and on by themselves. During the investigation they caught some electronic voice phenomena (EVP) as well as sounds coming from the ship's public address system.

USS *TORSK*

The USS *Torsk* is a Tench class submarine whose keel was laid on June 7, 1944. She served on the Pacific during World War

II and was nicknamed the "Galloping Ghost of the Japanese Coast." She is famous for sinking the last Japanese warship during World War II and for setting the all-time record for career dives with 11,884.

It was during one of these dives her ghost story began. On January 4, 1945, Joseph Grant Snow was accidentally left outside during a training dive. According to the log entry, "Snow, Joseph Grant, S1c, 884 75 80, USNR was found missing from his station. A thorough search of the ship was made but he was not found. An investigation was conducted by the Commanding Officer to determine the cause of the disappearance of Snow . . . It was determined that Snow was probably lost overboard on the sixth dive on 4 January."

His body was never recovered. He was the only serviceman to die on the *Torsk* during wartime. Legend says his ghost is still trying to get back into the submarine. His ghost has also been detected near the bunks where a shrine in his honor has been erected.

PRIDE OF BALTIMORE II
700 Lighthouse Point East #330, Baltimore, 21224

The original *Pride of Baltimore* was a reproduction of a nineteenth-century Baltimore clipper. It was designed to be a goodwill ambassador for the city and the state of Maryland. Sadly it was lost at sea on May 14, 1986, along with four of its twelve crew members.

A replica was commissioned in 1988 and is known as the *Pride of Baltimore II*. It was owned by the citizens of Maryland until 2010, when ownership was transferred to the private nonprofit organization running it. There are claims that the four crew members who were lost on the original *Pride* now haunt the *Pride II*. However, nothing more than odd footsteps have been heard on the ship.

Chapter 4
Fort McHenry

Best known for defending Baltimore during the War of 1812 and inspiring "The Star-Spangled Banner," Fort McHenry is a star-shaped fort surrounded by a dry moat. It is named after James McHenry, a signer of the US Constitution. The fort was one of the first to embrace its paranormal side. It gave ghost tours in the 1970s. Then someone decided they didn't want the ghosts to overshadow the history, and they were discontinued. But that hasn't stopped the ghosts from making their presence known.

Fort McHenry is most famous for inspiring Francis Scott Key to write "The Star-Spangled Banner" during the War of 1812. The star-shaped fort defended Baltimore Harbor from the British Navy on September 13 and 14, 1814. The battle resulted in several lives lost and created at least two of the ghosts at the fort.

During the battle a bomb exploded on the gun emplacement Bastion 3, resulting in the deaths of Levi Clagett and Sergeant John Clemm. (Two other men died during the battle, Privates Charles Messenger and Thomas V. Beason. How and where they died is unclear, but it is possible they also died at Bastion 3.) Since that night in 1814, people have seen a man walking along Bastion 3, now known a "Clagett's Bastion."

Park rangers have reported seeing an indistinct figure of a man walking along Bastion 3. Visitors have also reported seeing a man dressed in a uniform like that worn in the

1800s. Most think initially that he is a reenactor, until the man vanishes.

Another casualty of the battle was Private William Williams. Some sources state he is one of the four men who died during the battle, but according to records at the National Archive, Williams had been severely wounded during the battle after his leg was blown off by a cannonball. He was taken to the garrison hospital at Fort McHenry, where he died from his wounds.

Williams has an interesting backstory. Apparently he was a runaway slave named Frederick Hall. His owner, Benjamin Oden, placed an ad in newspapers in 1814 looking for him. He was described as "twenty-one years old, 5 feet 7 or 8 inches high, with a short chub nose and so fair as to show freckles."

Federal law prohibited slaves from entering into the military, because they legally could not enter into a valid contract. Apparently no one bothered to check when he enlisted on April 14, 1814. He was ordered to McHenry in September.

Williams's ghost has been seen a number of times. On the website ghostandstories.com, Robert J. tells of his experience with Williams's ghost on August 2007. He was on the bastion with his wife when he saw a "tall, dark figure marching with what looked like a gun on his shoulder on the path across from me about 15–20 feet away." Although he couldn't make out the man's features, he was certain the man was black. Robert knelt down to tie his shoe, and when he glanced up the man was gone. He looked all around, but he had vanished.

Others have also reported seeing a black man with a rifle on his shoulder walking back and forth as if on duty. As one of only a handful of black men who may have fought at Fort McHenry, and the only one on record who died at the fort, he is the likely source for the ghost.

An interesting footnote to Williams's story occurred in 1833–1824. Oden, petitioned the government for Williams's land bounty. Land bounties of 160 acres were given to veterans of the War of 1812. Apparently Oden felt he deserved the land, because he considered Williams his property. However, the government dismissed his claim for the same reason. As a slave, Williams could not own or acquire real estate; therefore, the bounty couldn't be given.

Another ghost who is still on duty is Private John Drew. Drew's story is told in Volume 18 of *The United States Army and Navy Journal and Gazette of the Regular and Volunteer Forces:*

> Private Drew . . . committed suicide at Fort McHenry, MD, on the morning of Nov. 15, [1880] by shooting himself in the head with a Springfield rifle. Mental disturbance, owing to being discovered sleeping at his post the night before, is said to have been the cause of his act. He had been ordered into a cell to await the commandant's orders, and while there blew his brains out, putting the muzzle of the rifle in his mouth, and pulling the trigger with the bared toe of his right foot. He was thirty-two years old, born in London, and had been several years in service. He was accorded a soldier's burial [at] Loudon Park Cemetery.

His ghost has been seen both in his cell and in the area where he fell asleep. People have reported seeing a man wearing a soldier's cape pacing back and forth along the outer battery where Drew was found sleeping.

In the late 1970s a local psychic named Dorothy Bathgate visited the fort with the director of visitor services, Warren Bielenberg. According to Bielenberg, Bathgate had mentioned seeing John Drew on the outer battery, but he was unable to see anything. Finally Bielenberg said, "John, if that's you, send us a message."

Bielenberg said, "I'll swear on this until the day I die that there [came] a tap like a fingernail at the window of the guard house. It came from 15 feet in front of me, and I couldn't see anything making the noise."

On another occasion a park ranger was walking his dog near the area where Drew had been found asleep. As soon as they reached that spot, the dog began growling and its hair stood up. Then the dog turned and ran, as if to escape something only it could see.

Virginia Lamkin wrote on the blog "Seeks Ghosts" that a docent working in the fort shared a story about when she was working in the prison cells. The docent felt like he wasn't alone, so he decided that the ghost of George William Brown was with him. Brown was imprisoned at Fort McHenry during the Civil War. He was the mayor of Baltimore from 1860 until 1861. When martial law was declared in Baltimore in 1861, he and several other officials sympathetic to the Confederacy were arrested. He was later released.

The docent would often talk to "George" and always made a point to tell him good night before he left. One day, in his rush to leave, he forgot. As he walked up to the cell door to exit, it slammed shut. He attempted to open it, but it slammed shut again and he felt hands pushing him away from the door. Finally he realized what he had done and said, "Good night, George." The cell door slowly opened, and the docent made a hasty retreat.

Since George did not die at Fort McHenry and no other ghost stories are associated with him at the fort, one has to wonder if this might have been John's ghost, and not George's.

Not all the ghosts at Fort McHenry are friendly and protective. A woman in white has attacked several people. She has been seen on the second floor of a building that was once enlisted men's quarters.

An artist at the fort was in this area when he was struck in the head and knocked unconscious. When he awoke, he was confused. He knew he had not bumped his head against the doorframe (which was low) and no one else had been in the area. Plus, he had no bumps or bruises on his head.

When the park ranger escorting him returned, the ranger told him it must have been the ghost. Apparently the ranger had his own experience with her. He had been pushed down the stairway by a woman dressed in nineteenth-century clothing. The ghost is believed to be the wife of a sergeant. After she lost all of her children to cholera or typhoid, she went insane.

Other ghostly phenomena that have been reported in the fort include hearing heavy footsteps, crying, and drums being played. People have reported smelling gunpowder. Others report that furniture has been moved, lights turn on and off, and doors open on small shut-in areas that had been unoccupied. Cold spots are also felt in buildings, even though the heat is turned on, and voices have been heard by employees after the fort has been closed. Many people also say they feel "a sense of dread" or "that they are being watched" when in the fort.

Then there is the 1974 report that seems to support the hauntings. The fort was being checked out by the Secret Service in preparation for President Gerald Ford's visit. The fort had been locked down and cleared of visitors when they spotted a man dressed in a uniform standing on one of the porches.

The fort used to embrace its ghosts and even gave ghost tours long before it was popular. But about twenty years ago, officials decided they didn't want McHenry to become known as the "Haunted Fort" and stopped all tours and discouraged park rangers from discussing them.

Chapter 5

Elsewhere in Baltimore

Not all of Baltimore's ghosts are centered near Poe and the waterfront. There are a few ghosts elsewhere, like the friendly ghost at Club Charles and the not-so-friendly ghost next door. The Lord Baltimore Hotel has several ghosts haunting its rooms. And no Baltimore ghost section would be complete without talking about Green Mount and Druid Ridge Cemeteries.

CLUB CHARLES
1724 North Charles Street, Baltimore, 21201

Club Charles was opened in 1951 by Esther West. It was originally named the Wigwam, but the name was changed in 1981. It eventually was purchased by Joy Martin.

Edward "Frenchie" Nate was a regular at the bar. He worked as a waiter at an exclusive restaurant and was always seen wearing a tuxedo-like uniform. He claimed to have been a double agent for the allies during World War II who later immigrated to Baltimore. It seems he enjoyed the bar so much, he decided to never leave.

Lysa McLane, a bartender at Club Charles, was interviewed for the show *Haunted Baltimore*. On the show she said, "I used to see someone standing at the top of the stairs all the time. A man. And I kept thinking it was my imagination because there was no one else in here." She finally mentioned it to her boss, who informed her about the ghost.

On another night, McLane had set a beer aside to enjoy after she had finished closing. She went downstairs to ask her boss a question. When she returned, the bottle was sitting at the end of the bar, open, with a glass next to it. She knew Frenchie had to have done it.

The ghost has also been known to turn on the taps, cause glasses to fly off the bar shelves, and appear in the men's room mirror. He also likes to rearrange the takeout liquor cabinet. According to McLane, he does this every night and every time the bottles are moved in a different manner.

THE ZODIAC

1726 NORTH CHARLES STREET, BALTIMORE, 21201

The Zodiac was the sister restaurant to Club Charles. When Joy Martin was renovating the building in 1989, she found a stash of liquor bottles under the floor. She believes the location may have been a speakeasy during Prohibition.

The ghost frequently appeared at table 13. He was described as a man wearing 1920s clothing that included a white linen vest and pants, a white shirt, a bowtie, and a straw hat. He smoked a cigar, and many smelled the faint odor of cigar smoke. Waiters unfamiliar with the ghost often went to the table to take his order, only to find the table empty.

A local resident told the owner that the location used to be a speakeasy run by an unpleasant man named McKim. After his wife left him, the man hanged himself in the basement. Apparently death did not improve his mood any.

Employees were particularly nervous about going to the storage room on the stairs. Many reported nearly falling down the stairs. They also got a feeling of dread or felt like they were being watched in this area. Some even heard a mysterious voice telling them to "Get out!" Doors were known to slam shut.

The Zodiac closed in 2008 and eventually became the Yellow Sign Theatre. Perhaps the change in venue has improved McKim's spirits, as no new reports of the building being haunted have emerged since the change.

LORD BALTIMORE HOTEL
20 WEST BALTIMORE STREET, BALTIMORE, 21201

In 1998 Fran Carter was preparing a nineteenth-floor meeting room for an event when she saw a little girl run past the open doorway bouncing a red ball. The girl was wearing a long, cream dress and black shoes. Fran went to the door and called out, "Little girl, are you lost?" but the hallway was empty. She turned to go back to work, when she saw an older man in a suit with a woman wearing a long ball gown. She asked them if they were looking for their grandchild and then turned and pointed in the direction she'd seen the girl running. When she turned back the couple had vanished too.

Fran immediately called a security guard to stay with her until she was finished. Years later a guest approached Fran, claiming her room had a ghost. The guest had awoken in the middle of the night after hearing a child crying. When she sat up, she saw a little girl rocking herself back and forth near the window. Before she could approach, the child vanished. The girl was wearing a cream dress and black shoes.

According to hotel staff, the elevator frequently travels to the nineteenth floor without being called. When it returns to the lobby, no one is inside. Guests and employees have complained that they have felt as if someone was touching them when riding in the elevator.

It is thought the girl may have committed suicide in the hotel. Guests have also reported feeling a presence in their rooms or awaken after having nightmares. And while no reports exist of a young girl having committed suicide at the Lord Baltimore, quite a few other people have.

In 1931 Mrs. Gertrude Merriken, thirty-four years old, committed suicide using a pistol in one of the rooms after the man she was seeing refused to marry her. In 1939 Edith Lansburgh, fifty-eight years old, fell or jumped from the sixteenth floor of the hotel. In 1946 Air Force Captain Elmer Bryan, thirty years old, jumped from the fourteenth floor of the hotel. In 1955 Edgar Fassburg committed suicide after taking a barbiturate. In 1966 retired Air Force Brigadier General Lacey Van Buren shot himself in the chest at the hotel.

Three other ghosts also have been seen in the ballroom of the hotel. They were standing near the windows when an employee reported it to Fran. When Fran investigated, she saw two men, one at the far left window and the other at the far right window, and a woman a few feet behind them near the middle window. Fran went into the room and switched on the light, and the three figures had vanished.

GREEN MOUNT CEMETERY
1501 GREENMOUNT AVENUE, BALTIMORE, 21202

Green Mount Cemetery was dedicated in 1839. It has become the final resting place of over sixty-five thousand bodies, including a number of Civil War generals and prominent figures from Baltimore's history. Located on sixty-five acres in northern Baltimore, the cemetery has two graves that must be mentioned.

The Ouija Board is often mentioned in ghost books, but the device has a strong connection to the Green Mount Cemetery. On February 10, 1891, patent lawyer Elijah Bond was awarded a patent for a new "toy or game" that mysteriously answered questions about the past, present, and future. According to legend, the patent officer refused to award Bond the patent unless he could prove that it worked by spelling out the officer's name, which was unknown to Bond. The board did, and Bond got his patent.

Initially the Ouija Board was treated like a harmless game. The May 1, 1920, issue of the *Saturday Evening Post* depicted a Norman Rockwell illustration of a man and woman playing the device. An episode of *I Love Lucy*, a show that couldn't use the word "pregnant" or show a married couple sleeping in the same bed, showed Lucy and Ethel using the board to host a séance.

It wasn't until the 1970s, after the Ouija Board was featured in the movie *The Exorcist*, that people's feelings about the device changed. By the 1980s a number of horror movies featured the board as a prime catalyst for ghosts and hauntings, although stores still stock it with their board games, as does Amazon.com.

Despite the success of the Ouija Board, Bond was buried in an unmarked grave in Green Mount Cemetery after he died on April 14, 1921. For more than eighty-five years, his grave lay unmarked until an Ouija Board enthusiast, Robert Munch, finally located it. According to Munch, he spent fifteen years trying to locate the exact grave. (If only there was a device that would have allowed him to contact Bond's ghost . . .)

Munch, with the financial assistance of numerous other Ouija Board enthusiasts, installed a gravestone above Bond's grave. On one side is the traditional engraving of names and dates. On the other side is a copy of a Ouija Board taken from Bond's original patent.

Another unmarked grave in the Green Mount Cemetery belongs to John Wilkes Booth, Abraham Lincoln's assassin. After Booth shot Lincoln, he fled south. He was eventually found and shot in Caroline County, Virginia. His body was brought to Fort Lesley McNair and buried beneath the prison floor wrapped in an army blanket. In 1869 the body was exhumed, placed in a pine box, and placed in a locked storeroom in Warehouse I at the prison. Two years later the body was released to the Booth family and buried in the family plot. The grave was never marked. Visitors to the plot often mistake a small white stone as being the gravestone of John Wilkes Booth. However, this is more likely the footstone to another grave. That doesn't stop visitors from placing pennies on the stone, however, either as a tribute to Booth or as a final snub because the penny contains Lincoln's likeness.

Only one ghost story has been recorded about Green Mount. According to legend the cemetery lies on land that once belonged to Robert Oliver. One dark and stormy night, Oliver's daughter dressed in masculine clothing to sneak out to meet her lover. Her father, not recognizing her, shot and killed her, mistakenly believing she was an intruder. In his despair Oliver vowed his estate would be turned into a cemetery in her memory. Her ghost is said to walk among the tombstones to this day.

One problem exists with this story, however: Oliver did have several daughters, but they died of old age or natural causes. Not one of them was shot. If a female ghost walks the grounds, it is not the daughter of Robert Oliver.

DRUID RIDGE CEMETERY
7900 Park Heights Avenue, Baltimore, 21208

In 1907 Felix Agnus purchased a statue to adorn his family plot in Druid Ridge Cemetery. It was the statue of a figure draped in cloth. Its face was shadowed by a hood, and its right arm reached up to touch its chin. While striking, nothing about it suggested it was anything but a statue.

It wasn't even a unique piece, but a copy of a piece Henry Adams had commissioned for his wife's grave. The piece was created by Augustus Saint-Gaudens. Agnus's copy wasn't authorized, however, but Agnus refused to remove it even after Adams and Saint-Gaudens sued.

The sculpture stayed. Felix Agnus passed away on Halloween in 1925. As the years went by, the statue was nicknamed "Black Aggie." Unlike the original, which seemed harmless, Black Aggie turned sinister after Agnus died.

People said nothing would grow in the statue's shadow. Pregnant women experienced miscarriages after passing under its shadow. At midnight the statue's eyes would glow red. It was this last legend that led local fraternities to use the statue during initiations. Pledges would need to spend the night sitting on Aggie's lap. Some say one such pledge suffered a heart attack in his attempt and was found next to the statue the following morning.

As Black Aggie's legend grew, so did the crowds it drew. Vandalism and partying in the cemetery became a huge problem in the 1960s. In 1962 one of Aggie's arms was cut off. It was later found in back of a truck. According to the truck owner, Aggie had cut off her own arm and given it to him in a fit of grief. (The judge found him guilty anyway.)

Finally cemetery officials had enough. In 1967 the statue was removed. For twenty years she disappeared. Then, in the late 1980s, she was placed in the courtyard of the Federal Judicial Center in Washington DC where she remains until this day.

Part 2

ANNAPOLIS

Annapolis is the capital of Maryland and located about thirty miles from both Baltimore and Washington DC. Situated on the Chesapeake Bay at the mouth of the Severn River, Annapolis has strong maritime roots and unique ghost stories—such as the story of a mother who took on the Navy after seeing her son's ghost, the headless ghost that wanders the street, or the gravedigger still digging graves after all these years.

Chapter 6

Annapolis Legends

In Annapolis, the ghosts are not all confined to buildings. At least two wander around near St. Anne's Church and Cornhill Street, which is just two blocks away. You'll have to decide if Joe Morgue or the headless ghost is scarier. For most, it's a toss-up. Then there is the ghost in the State House who refuses to accept his own death.

ST. ANNE'S CHURCH
199 Duke of Gloucester Street, Annapolis, 21401

When driving around St. Anne's Church at night, check out the yard surrounding the church and you might catch a glimpse of Joseph Simmons. Simmons has white hair and a long white beard. He's not known for his cleanliness. His clothing is old, baggy, and ragged, and he appears to need a good, long shower. Oh, he also happens to have been dead since 1829.

Simmons was a gravedigger before his death with, as his obituary says, "peculiarities of character." He loved his job. If he didn't have a grave to dig, he was known to dig up previous burials and redo the job. On one occasion a man he was burying had the ill grace to awaken in the coffin. Simmons refused to stop burying him. When the bystanders tried to stop him, Simmons responded, "Well, he's got to die sometime, and if he was not dead, he ought to be." Simmons had to be pulled away by the man's funeral party. When the man finally did pass away, Simmons refused to dig his grave out of spite.

Townspeople nicknamed him "Joe Morgue," a name he detested. If a child made the mistake of calling him "Mr. Morgue," Simmons would dig a child-size grave in the child's yard as if to say, "You're next." If an adult offended him, he or she learned to avoid Simmons or hear him mutter, "I'll have you someday" whenever they passed by him.

Death hasn't changed Simmons demeanor much. His figure is often seen walking on Northeast Street toward Church Circle, the commute he used to make each day to work. He likes to hang out around St. Anne's Church. Police report getting calls about a "homeless person" matching Simmons's description seen digging in the cemetery around the church, although nothing is ever disturbed. He likes to hang out on the western side of the church and is sometimes seen leaning against his shovel. He has also been seen sitting in the last pew of the church, only to quickly leave out the front the minute someone sees him.

People walking around the church at night have reported hearing whispers (sometimes he whispers their names), walking through cold spots, and seeing lights moving about the empty church. Tour guides say the street lights around the church flicker, which wouldn't be that odd except that the lights seem to do it in response to special moments of their stories. Some even claim to have felt Simmons tugging on their ears and clothing.

GHOST HORSE

The May 19, 1949, edition of *The Capital* reported people had been awoken by the sound of rattling and seen a ghost loaded down with chains galloping down the street. The ghost appeared when the clock in the tower at St. Anne's struck twelve. The horse would then disappear into the river.

MARYLAND STATE HOUSE
100 STATE CIRCLE, ANNAPOLIS, 21401

For years people have reported seeing a mysterious figure wandering the grounds of the capitol building, usually near the building dome. The figure is described as wearing eighteenth-century clothing, with a cocked hat over a long ponytail, and sporting a long-stemmed pipe. Many people assume he's a tour guide dressed in historic costume and have even approached employees to inquire about the tour. Others complain to security guards about the reenactor smoking a pipe in the nonsmoking building. They are startled to discover that there is no tour and no reenactors—just one ghost.

The Maryland State House is the third building built on that spot. Its cornerstone was laid on March 28, 1772, but a hurricane and the Revolutionary War delayed construction so much so that the project was abandoned in 1779 with the building only half-done. In 1784 Joseph Clark, a local architect and builder, took on the task to finish the building plus repair the roof and dome. He completed the exterior work in 1788, but the interior would take another nine years.

The project was marred by one tragedy. On Saturday, February 23, 1793, Thomas Dance fell ninety feet from the upper scaffold of the dome. The February 28, 1793, *Maryland Gazette* reported that he died a few hours later. Died, but didn't leave.

According to legend, Dance doesn't haunt the building because he died there. He's upset over the way his family was treated. His wife and family were denied payment of his pension and outstanding salary. The contractor in charge confiscated Dance's work tools, which created an additional hardship on the family. As if that wasn't enough, his family was then forcefully deported back to England. But if Dance is an angry ghost, he doesn't really show it.

He likes to lean over the railing of the inside balcony that circles the crown of the dome on the eastern-facing side or around the exterior balcony. Many attribute the sudden blasts of cold air that bedevil the building to Thomas. The drafts are known to scatter papers and even knock over small objects. Footsteps echo through empty corridors, lights turn off and on, and doors open and close, all without any visible cause. Security guards frequently respond to false alarms in one area of the building only to have another alarm (also false) ring in the opposite end of the building.

Then there are the objects that move without any cause. The tally on the voting board has been changed. Pitchers of water are knocked over. Some even claim to have seen objects floating in midair.

Employees responsible for flying the building's flags report feeling a "presence" nearby when on the exterior walkways near the dome. That same feeling—that they were not quite alone—is a common complaint among employees who have worked in the building.

And while Dance seems to lean more toward pranks than maliciousness, many cautionary tales exist about those who anger him. Dance is protective toward the dome that he gave his life to finish and doesn't appreciate people who claim he doesn't exist. He responds to them by sending a blast of cold air strong enough to open doors, rattle the windows, and even knock people over. He did it to a group of tourists in July 1997 after one of them made negative comments about the dome. The man was so startled, he ran out of the building never to return.

HEADLESS GHOST OF CORNHILL STREET

The story begins with an average colonial family that lived on Cornhill Street during late 1700s. One summer an epidemic of smallpox hit Annapolis. The parents died of the disease, but their two sons survived. The oldest son was old enough to serve as guardian of the younger son, and the two continued to live in their family home.

Without parental guidance, however, the behavior of the boys declined. They spent their time and money in local taverns and brothels. When the taverns closed for the night, they moved the gathering into their home, disrupting the peace and quiet of the neighborhood. Eventually the neighbors had had enough and decided to talk to the boys.

When they arrived at the house, only the younger boy was there. He claimed his brother had gone to Baltimore and promised the partying would stop. True to his word, the house was quiet. And while they frequently saw the younger boy coming and going, the older boy was nowhere to be seen.

For a brief time all was good. But a few days later, a horrible stench was detected on the street. Every day the odor grew worse. It appeared to be coming from the boys' house. A few neighbors decided to investigate and discovered a shallow grave in the cellar with a headless body inside.

They confronted the younger brother. He immediately confessed to burying his brother's body in the basement. The two had had a fight while drunk. During the fight the older brother fell, hitting his head and breaking his neck. The younger boy panicked and rather than seeking help, he decided to cover it up. His brother was big, too big for him to carry out of town undetected.

He decided the only way to get rid of the body was piece by piece. He removed his brother's head and carried it to the nearby harbor for disposal. He figured even if it was discovered there, everyone would assume he had met with foul play or an accident, and no one would suspect him.

After disposing of the head, the brother had sobered up considerably. Sober, he didn't have the heart or stomach to continue his task. So he buried the rest of the body in the basement. The young man was found guilty of manslaughter and sentenced to jail.

A new family moved into the house. All was quiet on the block until the guilty brother died in prison. That night, the family was awoken by the sound of heavy footsteps clomping up the basement steps, then down the hall and out the front door. When the family investigated, they discovered the basement and front door open, but no one on the street.

Since that night Cornhill Street has been bedeviled by a headless ghost roaming the area. In the 1880s, Thomas Chaney claimed his seventeen-year-old son, Thomas Jr., was approaching the Spa Creek Bridge when he saw a figure walking behind him. Thinking it was his father, he paused for a closer look, only to discover to his horror the figure did not have a head. He immediately took off for home. However, no matter how fast he ran, the headless figure kept pace and even seemed to gain on him. It moved with a strange, gliding gate as if it was floating rather than walking.

Thomas made it to his house, but as he moved to open the door, he felt a cold hand on his shoulder accompanied by a foul odor. His mother, having heard a commotion, opened the door. Her son knocked her down in his effort to get inside. He quickly slammed the door and ran for his father's gun. Then he opened the door, intent on confronting the creature. But the front yard and the street were completely empty.

A fisherman also reported seeing the headless ghost after World War II. He was preparing to head out for the day when he saw a figure stumbling around the docks. Concerned that the man had had too much to drink and might fall in, he decided to leave his boat and offer the man some help. But as he got closer to the figure, he realized the man didn't have a head. He let out a scream and then ran back to his boat. He quickly cast off, managing to make it before the figure reached him.

When the fisherman recounted his tail to friends later, they laughed at him—until another man admitted his son had encountered a similar figure a year earlier on Green Street. The son had also thought the man was drunk based on the way he was stumbling around, until he saw the body had no head. The boy freaked out and started running back the way he came. When he glanced behind him, he discovered the figure was speeding after him. Again it was no longer stumbling, but gliding along the way Thomas Jr. had described it. The figure continued to chase after the boy until he made it to Main Street and ran into a group of people.

Another account of the ghost was published in *The Capital* in 1949. According to the article, the headless man was seen walking down Green Street to Market Space, but that it hadn't been seen since the Spanish-American War. The last time it was seen was when a soft-crabber was heading to work one morning. As soon as he saw the ghost, he started running back toward his home. But when he arrived home, the headless man was waiting for him on his doorstep. The soft-crabber immediately fainted.

Legend says the ghost is looking for the head his brother took from him. If he catches you, he'll drag you into Spa Creek and force you to help him look for it.

Others claim the headless ghost is Charles Legg. Legg died in a fire on October 23, 1883. He ran into the fire to save his aunt, but was killed when the floor collapsed. They found his body, headless, after the fire was extinguished.

According to a newspaper account published on October 24, 1883, "The charred remains of Miss Lizzie Watkins and Mr. Charles Legg, who were burned here yesterday, were found this morning. From the position of the remains, Mr. Legg had reached his aunt on the third story, and was on his way out of the house when he was overcome by smoke or fire." No mention is made of him having fallen through the floor or his body being headless.

Chapter 7

Naval Academy

The US Naval Academy was established in 1845 and built where Fort Severn once stood. It is also the burial place of a naval legend, John Paul Jones. It took a lot of effort to bring Jones to Annapolis after he died, but if his ghost is any indication, he recognizes the effort. Then there is the story of James Sutton Jr., who died here in 1907 but still continues to haunt it. Some say he hasn't left because his murderer was never brought to justice, although the Navy still insists he committed suicide. Sutton's ghost appeared to several members of his family shortly after his death, spurring them to take on the Navy to uncover the truth.

JAMES SUTTON JR.

At 1:30 a.m. on October 13, 1907, Second Lieutenant James "Jimmy" Sutton Jr. was shot in the head. He died a few minutes later from his wound. That is about all that is agreed on about his death. Several naval officers who were with Sutton at the time claim that he pulled the trigger himself. Sutton's mother, Rosa Sutton, claimed she had it on good authority that he was murdered. Who told her that? Her son, James Sutton.

Jimmy's ghost appeared first to his mother at the instant she received the news from his father. She felt his presence and then saw him reaching out his hands to her and swore he didn't commit suicide. Mrs. Sutton asked her husband and two daughters if they saw the ghost, but they didn't.

Losing a child is said to be one of the worst things a person can experience. The trauma of the event can break up marriages and cause people to become unhinged. The Suttons were Catholic. If their son committed suicide, it would mean his soul was condemned to hell forever. Obviously they would go to extraordinary lengths to deny it.

But what make Rosa's claims more believable are the details about her son's death that she shared with friends and family members. The Suttons, who lived in Portland, received a brief telegram about their son's suicide. Their daughter, Rose, had left for Annapolis to attend to details, but the train trip would take nearly a week. They had no access to information about their son's death other than the telegram. Despite this, Rosa knew:

Jimmy had been in a fight with several men.
One of the men was named Utley.
The men had beaten Jimmy and caused wounds on his forehead and a lump on his jaw.
His head wound was wrapped with a bandage that had been tied around the nape of his neck.
His watch had been smashed.
His body was placed in a basement after his death and left there unattended.
His uniform was missing a shoulder knot.
The gun that shot him wasn't his.

All of these came from several "visions" she had of her son. She never referred to Jimmy as being a ghost. She relayed the details of her sightings to a number of people.

All of them confirmed the details Rosa told them when the matter was investigated by the American Society for Psychical Research in 1910.

But it wasn't just his mother that Jimmy appeared to. His sister and aunt also claimed to have seen him. According to Robin R. Cutler in her book about the case, *A Soul on Trial,* Jim Sutton told the press that his wife, daughter, and sister, Margaret Ainsworth, had all seen Jimmy in their dreams on October 15, 1907. In this dream Jimmy was wearing a white shirt and told them he had been struck by a gun. Jim said, "The inquiry has shown that he was in shirt sleeves and wore such a bandage when buried as my wife had dreamed."

The Court of Inquiry found "Lieutenant Sutton is directly and solely responsible for his own death which was self-inflicted, either intentionally or in an effort to shoot one of the persons restraining him and his death was not caused by any other injury whatever." It should be pointed out that Sutton had been shot about three inches above his right ear, and an expert had testified that it would have been impossible for Jimmy to have fired the shot.

While this didn't satisfy the Suttons, it was enough to satisfy the Catholic Church. When Jimmy's body was exhumed for a second autopsy, a priest blessed his grave. The end of the inquiry also ended Rosa's visions of her son. She reportedly never saw his spirit again. That doesn't mean Jimmy's soul found rest. It seems Jimmy has moved to haunt where he died.

Those who have spent the night in Bancroft Hall report being awoken by a cold draft. When they open their eyes, they see Jimmy's ghost hovering over their beds.

Security on the campus along King George Street was also increased after several people reported seeing a figure walking along (and sometimes through) the brick wall that separates the campus from the road. This happens to be the area where Jimmy died.

JOHN PAUL JONES

John Paul Jones was a Revolutionary War hero and a founder of the US Navy. His actions in British waters during the Revolution helped win the war and made him a legend. It was he who said, "I have not yet begun to fight," during a clash with the British warship *Serapis*. In 1797 he joined the Russian Navy but left after two years. He then went to Paris where he tried, unsuccessfully, to rejoin the Russian Navy. He died in Paris at the young age of forty-five on July 18, 1792. He was buried in a Paris cemetery.

For over one hundred years, Jones's burial in Paris didn't seem to bother anyone. Then, at the turn of the twentieth century, people suddenly seemed bothered that an American hero was buried in France. In the summer of 1899, the secretary of state contacted Henry Vignaud, US ambassador stationed in Paris, to inquire about the state of John Paul Jones's grave. Vignaud admitted he'd been unable to locate the grave.

In 1901 it was discovered that Jones was buried in a small urban cemetery in Paris that had been abandoned. Buildings were built over the location, but the bodies were never moved. For the next several years, efforts were made to exhume the bodies; but because it would require demolishing at least one, if not more, buildings, authorities were reluctant, as it would be hard to establish the identity after over one hundred years.

But a new ambassador, Horace Porter, was determined to find Jones. Rather than demolishing the buildings, he proposed digging tunnels underneath them. Digging began in mid-February 1905. Almost immediately success seemed at hand when on February 24 a lead casket was uncovered. However, it ended up being an American who died two years before Jones. For two months the search continued with no progress. On April 6, newspapers reported that a Mrs. Preston claimed Jones's mother had had him dis-interred shortly after his death and reburied in a cemetery in Dumfries, Scotland. A week later Porter announced that Jones's body had been found in Paris, not Scotland. Ironically the body had been found the day after Preston's claim, but it had taken authorities a week to confirm the identity of the grave.

With big fanfare Jones's body sailed across the Atlantic Ocean from France to the United States. But after all the effort to locate and discover Jones's body, no one had a plan on what to do with the body once it was found. No money was set aside for a tomb or new burial spot. The body was put where you put things that don't have a home: a storage room in the basement. It sat there for a year. Then it was dug out (literally) for a "Welcome Home" ceremony. After the ceremony the body was shuttled back to the basement. It wasn't until January 26, 1913, that it was moved to the marble sarcophagus on the lower level of the Naval Academy Chapel in Annapolis.

According to academy tradition, the ghost of John Paul Jones has been known to whisper advice to midshipmen. His advice would tell them how to be a good naval officer or what course their career should take. First class midshipmen used to stand vigil over his crypt in the hopes that such an incident would occur.

Both a tall figure wearing a hat and a shadowy figure have also been seen standing near Jones's sarcophagus. Electrical equipment also malfunctions in this area, and lights turn on and off. Pictures taken in the area often contain orbs or a strange mist.

Chapter 8
Annapolis Inns and Taverns

While in Annapolis you can eat and sleep with ghosts. The Maryland Inn has ghosts on every floor, so make sure you indicate if you want a "haunted" or "not haunted" room when you check in. Once you've checked in, check out some of the ghosts at the local establishments. A flirty ghost haunts the Rams Head, while the Reynolds and Middleton Taverns have former employees keeping the new staff hard at work.

THE MARYLAND INN
16 CHURCH CIRCLE, ANNAPOLIS, 21401

Employees working the graveyard shift in a hotel see a lot of odd things. A guest standing at the front desk dressed in nothing but pajamas and robe is not all that unusual. One night in the 1980s, the night clerk found just such a guest standing before him, looking extremely upset. Figuring she'd managed to lock herself out of her room, he was a little surprised to hear her request was not for an extra room key.

"I'd like you to find me a room with no dead people in it."

Apparently the guest was staying in a room on the fourth floor. All night she'd heard the sound of footsteps walking back and forth in the room. That didn't bother her.

Nor did it bother her that the window opened on its own after she had locked it. However, when she was awoken from a dead sleep by someone sitting on the bed, she had had enough. She wasn't paying good money to share her bed.

The fourth floor of the hotel is haunted by a ghost known only as the "bride." Legend says she was the long-time fiancée of a ship captain, Charles Campbell, in the early 1800s. After years of waiting Campbell was finally ready to give up sailing and settle down. In 1817 he wrote and asked his beloved to travel to Annapolis so they could get married.

On the day he was to arrive, she spent most of the day waiting for him in his room. She paced back and forth from the bed to the window to watch for his arrival. Early that afternoon she heard a commotion below and raced down the stairs out in the street. There lying in a bloody heap was her beloved, still in his naval uniform. He died in her arms.

Onlookers had to pry her away from the body to get it out of the street. Everyone was surprised when, rather than stay with the body, she walked back toward her hotel. Slowly she climbed the stairs back toward her room. A few minutes later the onlookers discovered why. She threw herself out her hotel window onto the street below. She landed within arm's reach of her beloved captain.

Ever since then she continues to haunt the room. Captain Campbell also haunts the hotel. He has been seen leaning against the main fireplace in the dining room. He's still dressed in his naval uniform and has side whiskers and a beard. He likes to enjoy a mug of beer and smoke his pipe. Sometimes he'll hold his mug up and wink with a smile on his face. People frequently spot him through the window. Some have been known to stop and complain to management about the reenactor breaking the "no smoking" laws that prohibit smoking in restaurants.

The Maryland Inn was built between 1772 and 1782. It has been almost continually used as either a boardinghouse or hotel since that time. Through the years, it has seen a lot of people in and out of its doors, and it seems some liked it so much they never left.

A 1920s-era ghost also haunts the fourth floor. Guests have heard the sound of two women arguing followed by the sound of a door slamming. When they look into the hall, they see a woman wearing a short, black beaded dress and a feather hair ornament. She is carrying her high heel shoes in her hand. She walks unsteadily to the stairwell. Next, the guests hear a shriek followed by something tumbling down the stairs. When the guests investigate, there is nothing the scent of perfume at the bottom of the stairs.

Another ghost haunts a room on the third floor. A woman was woken up in the middle of the night by the sound of a woman talking and calling her husband's name. She opened her eyes to see a woman in a pale nightgown looming over her. The woman looked enraged. The guest screamed and turned on the light, which awoke her husband and caused the spirit to disappear.

Other ghosts don't seem to have been given a room to haunt and are left to wander around the hotel. A group of Civil War infantry ghosts are heard going up the stairs to the second floor belting out bawdy songs. Another ghost likes to pass people on the stairway leaving the scent of roses behind. Others have reported being hit with a sudden gust of cold air on the stairway.

RAMS HEAD TAVERN
33 West Street, Annapolis, 21401

Having someone flirt with you in a bar is not that abnormal, unless you're at Rams Head Tavern. It starts with a noticeable cold spot. The temperature may drop as much as forty degrees below the surrounding area. A male visitor may then feel a hand gently caressing his face or hair, followed by soft, female laughter against his ear or the smell of strong, rose-scented perfume. Once the pattern is complete, Amy moves on to her next conquest. It's something she's been doing for decades, ever since she passed away.

Amy's backstory is mostly legend with little historical record to back it up. Long ago a sailor came into the tavern, which was also a brothel, looking for more than drink. He chose to spend the night with a young girl named Amy. In some stories she is the daughter of the tavern's widowed owner. They retired upstairs to a room above the bar. The man was particularly energetic, and before long, the rafters were shaking and the chandeliers were swaying, all to the delight of the bar's rowdy patrons.

Their delight turned to dismay when huge sections of plaster from the ceiling began raining down on them. As they dove under the tables to escape, the bed containing Amy and the sailor crashed through the ceiling. One of the bed posts caught in the plaster, spilling the two through the newly created hole onto the floor below. The sailor was injured, but survived. Amy's neck snapped, and she died instantly. To give credibility to the story, a bed post is stuck in the ceiling above the bar.

This story is sometimes placed near the time of the Civil War. However, John Washington Welsh Whittington purchased the property in 1831. Although he was a widower, all three of his daughters outlived him, and there is no historical record suggesting the location was a brothel during that time.

Before Whittington owned it, Keziah Lindsay Murrow Clark maintained a tavern, Sign of the Green Tree, which was run by Thomas Graham in 1790. Clark was widowed three times. Thomas Graham ran a newspaper advertisement announcing the opening of a "house of entertainment at the sign of the Green-Tree" to "give general satisfaction to all who please to favor him with their custom." It is believed that the Sign of the Green Tree was also a brothel, so it is possible that Amy was the daughter of either Clark or Graham. But nothing definitive exists to prove this.

But just because the legend associated with a ghost may not be truthful, it doesn't mean the location isn't haunted or the ghost doesn't exist. And enough people have encountered Amy to suggest she is more than a story.

While she's nice to the guys, she doesn't appreciate competition. She's been known to tip over chairs and spill drinks on women sitting near the object of her affection. She also targets females working in the building, as a former manager, Didi Dolan, described one evening when Amy was being particularly vexing.

As she and another female employee were trying to close, chairs kept falling off the tables and the phone rang incessantly with no one at the other end. But the last straw was when the adding machine started going off.

"The total button was being hit over and over again, and the tape was scrolling out the back," Dolan said in *Haunted*

Annapolis: Ghosts of the Capitol City. But when she and the other employee went over to investigate, she found the switch was clearly in the off position and the machine was unplugged. Breathy laughter filled the air, followed by a cool rose-scented breeze. The two women immediately left. After that night, they learned to ask a boyfriend or husband to hang out during closing to "entertain" Amy and keep her from pestering them.

However, men don't always have it easy at Rams Head. One busser, Eddie Hartman, told of an experience he had in the basement liquor cage. While he was down there, the whole cage started shaking. Was it Amy trying to get his attention or the ghostly soldier people claim haunts here?

A tall man dressed in a blue uniform with a cap is seen walking down the hallway toward the taproom or sitting quietly in the corner drinking a mug of beer. He is believed to be a Union soldier who may have passed away in the building. Perhaps he was out of liquor and wanted to get Hartman to pour him another one before he left for the night.

REYNOLDS TAVERN
7 Church Circle, Annapolis, 21401

Employees at Reynolds Tavern know they work for a hard-nosed manager. If they don't wipe down a table completely, she'll spill a flower vase or water pitcher across it, forcing them to do the job properly. If they don't set a table correctly, the silverware may be piled up in the center of the table. And if she doesn't like them, she's been known to break dishes and glasses in their presence.

And everyone knows not to use any foul language. Anyone—employee or guest—who swears too loudly has found liquids spilled on them and furniture tossed in their path. Guests report lights flicker when they curse, and if they continue, the lightbulb burns out.

This might seem like unconventional management techniques, possibly even harassing, but the employees have no choice but to either accept the working conditions or quit. You can't file a complaint against a manager who's been dead for over two hundred years.

William Reynolds built the tavern in 1747. After his death his third wife, Mary, continued to run the tavern. It was something she excelled at. She eventually passed away in 1785 and William's daughter, Margrette, continued to run it until 1796 when it was sold to John Davidson. It then became a boardinghouse followed by a residence and bank offices. It was almost demolished to become a gas station, but was saved and eventually restored back into a tavern in 1984.

Mary wasn't ready to leave her beloved tavern. The day she was buried, a relative reported walking into an upstairs room to see Mary sitting the end of her bed smiling. More sightings followed, and through the years the building was known for its odd happenings, but nothing significant until it became a tavern again.

She may be unconventional, but Mary is diligent. She's exposed several employees who attempted to steal from the tavern. One employee's backpack strap suddenly broke as he was leaving, causing his bag to crash to the floor and burst open. Inside were a bunch of frozen filet mignons. Other bags and purses have suddenly fallen to expose drugs, stolen wallets, and hidden cases of beer.

Guests who get a little too spirited or intoxicated learn to behave or face Mary's wrath. She'll start by knocking your drink in your lap. If you attempt to order more alcohol, she'll continue to knock it over. If you don't get the hint, she'll jostle your chair, knock food into you, or cause a cold draft to hit you—anything that will make you uncomfortable. If you still don't get the hint, she'll lock you into the bathroom. Patrons have been locked in the bathroom for thirty minutes after Mary got upset with them.

When she's not managing customers and employees, Mary has a more creative side. She's been heard whistling or singing in the kitchen and stairway, especially around Christmas. She also likes to set out cookbooks, ingredients, and spices onto the table—just her subtle way of suggesting menu changes.

MIDDLETON TAVERN
2 Market Space, Annapolis, 21401

Middleton Tavern was built in the 1750s. Its proximity to the State House made it a favorite among officials, resulting in a lot of historic names walking through its doors including George Washington, Ben Franklin, Thomas Jefferson, and the Marquis de Lafayette. Over the years it changed hands and identities a number of times before being restored to its original glory. Also, like most of the older buildings, it has a couple of resident ghosts.

"Roland" has been seen as both a shadowy figure floating from dining room to dining room and as a man dressed in colonial garb. He'll take dishes off the shelves and fling them around the room one at a time. When tables aren't cleared fast enough, he's been known to tip over the table—dishes and all. He rearranges furniture and turns wall lamps upside down. The smell of a cigar is also frequently smelled in the tavern, although cigar smoking is not allowed.

Another ghost, dressed in a Revolutionary War uniform, is frequently seen peering out the window. His identity is unknown and he disappears the instant someone approaches him. People describe him as looking longingly toward the harbor as if waiting for a ship to come in.

DOCK STREET BAR AND GRILL
136 DOCK STREET, ANNAPOLIS, 21401

The Dock Street Bar and Grill is located where the old Annapolis jail once stood before it was demolished in the 1910s. Since then a variety of taverns and restaurants have been built over the original jail's foundation, giving old ghosts a new place to haunt. Employees have reported hearing metal clanging, footsteps, coughs, and whispers in the building. Faces, moving lights, and full-bodied apparitions are seen on the first floor.

Chapter 9
Annapolis Houses

Historic houses in Annapolis are like castles in Europe: They aren't complete unless they have at least one ghost. However, some houses here might be considered ghost hoarders considering the number sighted there.

SHIPLAP HOUSE
18 Pickney Street, Annapolis, 21401

Francis Blackwell Mayer returned to Maryland in the 1870s after spending several years studying painting in Paris. He decided to purchase an older home known as the Shiplap House. Built around 1715, it was one of the oldest buildings in Annapolis. The name comes from the siding found on the rear of the house, which is usually used in shipbuilding. Mayer knew the house had originally been built as a tavern and thought the history would help inspire him. He also knew that the house was rumored to be haunted, but that didn't bother him. Over the years he frequently spotted a young woman wearing a light-colored dress moving about the interior of the house as well as the gardens. His neighbors also reported seeing her.

According to the neighbors, the ghost was of a young girl named Adrianne. She worked in the house when it was still a tavern. She was said to have been extraordinarily beautiful, which inspired jealousy in a number of potential suitors. One man became so jealous that he killed her when she rejected his affections. He figured if he couldn't have her, no one else could either. Although, that's only one of the tales of how Adrianne may have died.

Mayer lived peacefully with Adrianne until 1883, when he married a young widow, Ellen Benton Brewer. One night Mayer had retired early while his wife finished up some chores downstairs. He was just drifting off when he heard his wife walk up the stairs and enter the room. He turned toward her, but she didn't have a lamp, so all he saw was her feminine silhouette.

She pulled back the covers and got into bed. Mayer immediately noticed she was wearing an unfamiliar perfume and he complimented her on it. Oddly, she didn't respond. Fearing she was upset, he moved toward her and his feet brushed against hers. They were ice cold. Again he made a comment, but she made no response. Upset at her silence, Mayer lost his temper and shouted at her, "Are you going to lie there or are you going to answer me?"

From downstairs he heard his wife call out to him asking him what he wanted. Horrified, Mayer looked closer at the figure in bed beside him. It shifted restlessly and let out a mournful sigh. Mayer sprung out of bed with a shout and raced into the hallway. His wife immediately ran upstairs with a lamp in her hands. Mayer took the lamp from her and crept back into the bedroom. The bed was empty, except for an outline of a figure complete with a pillow indentation on his wife's side of the bed. Mayer and his wife moved out of the house soon after that.

Other couples who lived in the house had similar experiences. Husbands were often woken in the night feeling someone touching them in a provocative manner. When they turned toward what they thought were their wives, they discovered them still asleep and facing the opposite direction. One wife was changing the linens. She left the room to get clean sheets. When she returned, she found the word "Adrianne" written on the mattress cover in red lipstick.

The house eventually became the offices for the Historic Annapolis Foundation, but that doesn't mean Adrianne moved out. One employee was working late in her office on the second floor. She had made sure the house was locked up, so when she heard footsteps on the staircase she assumed it was a coworker. But no one responded when she called out a greeting. Cautiously, she peered out the doorway into the hall, only to find it empty.

Figuring it was her imagination, she went back to work, but again she heard footsteps on the stairs. This time they reached the top and then made their way into the office next to hers. Snatching up the phone, she tried dialing 911, but there was no dial tone. When she looked at it, she noticed all the extension lights were flashing as if they were being pressed.

Realizing she was on her own, she steeled herself to inspect the office next to hers. When she opened the door, a cool blast hit her. The room was freezing, but completely empty. As she stepped inside, she noticed that the buttons on the phone were depressed as if being pushed by an unseen finger. She gasped in horror, and it immediately stopped. She then heard footsteps on the wooden floor coming toward her from the desk. When they approached, two icy hands pushed her out of the way, and the footsteps continued on their way. It was the last time the employee worked late alone.

Two other ghosts also reside in the house. For years children occupying the house reported playing with a young girl named Audrey. Although no adults have ever seen her, numerous children have reported encounters with her. While one might be inclined to dismiss these accounts as childish imagination, the children have learned new games after playing with Audrey. One adult remembers how Audrey taught him how to play marbles. She is described as a five-year-old girl with yellow ringlets.

Audrey also has a nursemaid, although no one knows her name. She wears a dark dress with a white apron and tends to haunt the former nursery on the second floor. She's been known to tuck kids in at night or give them a swat on the butt if they misbehave.

JAMES BRICE HOUSE
42 East Street, Annapolis, 21401

The James Brice House is said to be the most haunted house in Annapolis. However, that seems to refer to the number of ghosts that haunt it and not the frequency of the hauntings. It could also be referring to how long it has been haunted. Stories have been published about the Brice House ghosts for almost one hundred years.

The house was started by John Brice II, but completed by his son James Brice. After James's death, his son Thomas inherited the house. Thomas lived the bachelor's life in the house. By all accounts he was a good man and well liked by his servants.

This is why it was a shock when Thomas was found dead in his study. It was unclear to authorities at the time if he was struck with a blunt object or if he had suffered a stroke and hit his head on the way down. However, when his valet disappeared the same night, they concluded it was murder.

Whatever the motive, Thomas Brice's ghost has been seen in the library. Some report seeing him and his manservant reenacting the murder. According to a 1949 article in *The Capital,* "Older Annapolitans said that the steps leading from the second floor to the attic creaked at night and at midnight the scuffle of feet and a shriek could be heard." It is believed that the ghosts are reenacting the murder. It also said that people had seen a specter walk through the open door of the governor's chamber and go out again.

But Thomas was not the first ghost at Brice House. Almost immediately after his death in 1801, James's wife, Juliana, reported seeing his ghost. His ghost is said to haunt the basement and one of the bedrooms. People also began hearing knocking. The knocking was described as sounding like Morse code.

William Oliver Stevens's 1937 book, *Annapolis: Anne Arundel's Town,* contains several stories about the ghosts experienced at Brice House. One story he shares came from a young man who was living on the top floor of the house and was surprised to see a black man walk through the open door of a room. The man then turned and walked out. The man got out of bed and ran to the hall, but the hall was empty.

Stevens also tells about a Naval Academy professor who lived on the first floor. As the professor passed the door to the library early one morning, he saw a man with white hair dressed in a black suit standing in the threshold. The man then "gradually melted out of sight like a mist." Another sighting occurred by a naval officer's wife and her daughter. No one knows if this is the ghost of Thomas or James Brice.

Another ghost described by Stevens is that of a young woman who appears at midnight. She is seen resting her elbows on the mantelpiece above the fireplace as if she may be weeping. She disappears in "wisps of vapor." Others have seen her hovering near the wine cellar. Those who have seen her say she looks right at them.

Another mystery of the Brice House occurred during one of the renovations when a closet was revealed. Inside the walls was the skeleton of a woman. Rumors say that the woman was a member of the Brice family who had been hidden away because she was insane. She was either buried in the walls after her death or entombed there when she was alive. The discovery was made in the 1890s.

However, people have heard a woman screaming, crying, and begging for help long before the skeleton was discovered. In recent years the police have been called by concerned passersby who are convinced some poor woman is trapped inside. The police investigate, but never find anyone.

A few other ghosts include a nursemaid and the arguing couple. The ghostly nursemaid haunts upstairs. She appears to be feeding and rocking infants as she did during her life. The ghostly couple was seen by Professor Alan Cook. He had gotten up in the middle of the night to make a cup of tea. Outside the kitchen window he observed a man and woman in the backyard. The woman was wearing a hoopskirt. The couple appeared to be having an argument. The man stomped into the house and was heard by Cook pacing back and forth, although Cook never saw the man enter the house.

GOVERNMENT HOUSE
110 State Circle, Annapolis, 21401

Reverdy Johnson was a complex individual. Although he opposed slavery, he represented the slave-owning defendant in *Dred Scott v. Sandford*. Then, while he was a US senator, he defended Mary Surratt before a military tribunal. At age seventy-nine, he was still practicing law. In February 1876 he traveled to Annapolis to argue a case before the Court of Appeals.

He stayed at the Government House as the guest of Governor Carroll. Carroll invited a number of guests over to meet Johnson. Dinner turned into a fairly rowdy party. Around 7:30, Johnson decided to go for a walk. He was found lying on the cobblestone carriageway. His body was taken down to the basement where it was examined. The doctor pronounced him dead. He had two large wounds to the right side of the head and a dislocated finger on the left hand. It was ruled an accidental death. The coroner figured that he either tripped or suffered an attack of vertigo.

Johnson's funeral was held in Baltimore about two weeks later, with Carroll in attendance. When he returned, he was told that there had been a number of strange occurrences at the house. Several people reported seeing a man who looked like Johnson near the house. They also heard music and voices coming from the reception room. Strange smells and lights were also experienced.

Paranormal encounters continued and still continue into present day. Guard dogs often balk at entering the room where the party was held. Staff claims that the activity increases around February 10, the day Johnson died. They try to avoid scheduling any events on that day in order to avoid unexplained events that might cause trouble.

BROOKSBY-SHAW HOUSE
21 State Circle, Annapolis, 21401

This house was Cornelius Brooksby's dream house, but he never got to live in it. He passed away a year before it was completed. His wife, Mary, remarried, and the couple moved into the house, which seemed to disturb Cornelius's ghost. They were immediately disturbed by phantom footsteps and the sound of glass breaking. One night the couple awoke to find the angry figure of Cornelius hovering over the bed. Mary's new husband, Thomas Gough, was poked by unseen hands, knocked down the staircase, and even had china and glasses thrown at him.

After several months of torment, the couple moved out. Eventually Cornelius's granddaughter, Mary Brooksby-Long, moved in. She also experienced paranormal phenomena and was forced to leave the house. The house was sold to John Shaw. While the Shaw family did have ghostly experiences, they were not tormented the way the previous occupants were and managed to stay. The house was eventually sold to the State of Maryland and houses legislative offices. By all accounts Cornelius still haunts the building. He seems to enjoy the Christmas season the most, and activity increases around that time.

Part 3

CENTRAL

Central Maryland contains both the state capital, Annapolis, and the largest city, Baltimore. It also has four cities with a high concentration of ghosts: Baltimore, Annapolis, Ellicott City, and Westminster. Some speculate that the granite located underneath the ground could be energizing the ghosts in this area. Or perhaps it is just the place to be when you're dead.

Chapter 10
Ellicott City

Ellicott City lies west of Baltimore and south of the Patapsco River. It has been listed in the top ten of Money *magazine's "Best Places to Live in the United States" numerous times. And apparently that holds true for both the living and the dead. Many consider Ellicott City one of the most haunted small towns on the East Coast (for those who consider sixty-four thousand people a "small" town).*

What makes this city so ghost-friendly (or Casper-esque) is probably not the hiking trails, great schools, or charming downtown, but something deeper beneath the surface: granite and granodiorite. Both of these rocks contain quartz, which is known for its electrical properties. Many believe ghosts need an energy source to manifest, which could explain why Ellicott City is a hotbed of paranormal activity.

DIAMONDBACK TAVERN
3733 OLD COLUMBIA PIKE, ELLICOTT CITY, 21043

The Diamondback Tavern has gone by a number of names, but its ghost has none other than "the lady in white." Some believe she was raped and murdered in the 1920s. Since her murderer was never caught, her soul can't find rest. Whoever she may be, she has made the Diamondback her home.

During renovations before it opened as the Tiber River Tavern, the owner came in one morning to discover footprints in the newly varnished floor. The footprints could only have been done after the building had been locked up. Another night the owner was closing up the bar for the night. He had already locked all the upstairs rooms, including a private dining room set up for an event the next day. While he was downstairs counting the money, he heard a loud crash. He raced upstairs and unlocked the dining room door. One of the tables had been completely flipped over with the chairs knocked back.

But what made the event stranger were the place settings. They weren't scattered or broken on the ground. Instead, they located exactly as they had been, just inverted. The only two doors into the room had been locked and the owner had the only key.

Another employee was closing for the night. He had extinguished all the candles and straightened the white tablecloths before going to find his general manager to tell him he was done. When the manager inspected the man's work, he was furious. The tablecloths were all messed up and some of the candles were still lit. The employee had no explanation and immediately left the building. Employees often feel a pressure on their backs, as if someone is tapping them, but when they look, no one is near them.

A cook working in the morning saw a woman with long hair wearing a white dress in the bar area. He followed the woman, but she disappeared after turning a corner. The cook immediately got the owner and the two searched the building. But no one else was inside and the doors were still locked. Two cops admitted to seeing a woman's face in an upper window. As they watched, the face slowly faded away.

Other employees have also described seeing a "lady in white" in the main dining room and hallways of the building.

JUDGE'S BENCH SALOON
8385 Main Street, Ellicott City, 21043

The Judge's Bench gets its name from when it was a mom-and-pop grocery store. Judges often walked from the courthouse to the store. They'd purchase a cold drink and sit on the benches in front of the store. The benches became known as the "judge's benches."

Legend says that while it was still a grocery store, the daughter of the proprietor committed suicide in the attic. She was either forbidden from seeing her sweetheart or had been wronged by her fiancé. They believe her name was Mary.

Mary likes to push liquor bottles off the shelves one by one behind the bar. She also makes noises on the upper floors when no one else is up there. She also causes the ladies' room toilet to flush on its own and spins the toilet paper roller.

Some stories mention Berger's Grocery as being the grocery store. Berger's Grocery was located at 8225 Main Street, and it burned to the ground on April 5, 1940. A theater was built in its place. The framework of the theater, which is now an antiques store, remains. At the time, Joseph and Mary Berger, both fifty-six years old, lived there alone with a boarder. No mention of them having a daughter or a Mary committing suicide has been uncovered.

LILBURN
3899 COLLEGE AVENUE, ELLICOTT CITY, 21043

In 1857 prosperous business owner Henry Richard Hazelhurst built Lilburn. He suffered several tragedies during his tenure in the house. Shortly after it was built, his daughter, Maria, died at age three. His second wife died in 1887. (His first wife died in 1848.) Three more daughters died in the 1890s. Catherine died in 1891 at age thirty-three. Julie died in 1893 at age thirty-one. Margaret died in 1895 at the age of thirty-six. By the time he died in 1900, Henry Hazelhurst had outlived most of his family.

Following his death, Hazelhurst's remaining children immediately sold the house to the Independent Order of Odd Fellows of Maryland. They owned it until 1923, when the Maginnis family purchased it. That same year, a fire broke out at Christmas, which destroyed a good portion of the house. John Maginnis rebuilt, but decided to make a change to the tower of the house and replaced the Gothic peaks with stone battlements. The change did not sit well with the former residents, because after this change the hauntings began.

The family began hearing the sound of footsteps walking through the house and climbing the tower stairs. Windows in the tower would open by themselves, sometimes refusing to close.

An interesting account of the footsteps was made by a police officer in 1975. He had gone to Lilburn to interview a victim of an armed robbery at a jewelry store. According to the officer, "I heard the sounds of footsteps on the floor above. I looked at the woman to see if she was going to react. (She was supposed to be the only one home.) She acted as if she didn't hear a thing. I asked her about the footsteps and she replied, 'Oh, that's just the poltergeist.'"

The woman told the officer that the ghost opened a belfry window during the winter. Her father responded by nailing the window shut, only to find the window wide open the following morning. Another resident tried tying the windows closed with heavy rope, only to find the windows open again when he stepped outside.

The footsteps and window opening may be caused by the ghost of Henry Hazelhurst. Some speculate he is unhappy with the changes in his house and making his displeasure known. On one occasion a male figure materialized in a doorway. Cigar smoke is also smelled and seen in the library of the house.

The ghost of a little girl also haunts Lilburn. She would likely be the ghost of Maria Hazelhurst, who died in the house. She has been heard crying in an upstairs bedroom. She wears a chiffon dress and has been seen in various rooms of the house. On one occasion she was seen walking hand in hand with a man, so maybe Henry and Maria have found each other.

The ghost of another of Henry's daughters may also haunt the house. She died while giving birth in the house. This would likely be the ghost of Julie who died two years after getting married, although it is unclear how or where she died. However, some say one of the spirits is named Margaret, which is the name of the daughter who died in 1895.

Margaret is blamed for most of the mischief in the house, such as the chandelier moving. It has been seen on several occasions swinging back and forth, then stopping, then swinging again. Another time, a witness reported seeing a vase of flowers rise off its stand and turn over, dumping water and flowers onto the floor.

HOWARD COUNTY COURTHOUSE
8360 Court Avenue, Ellicott City, 21043

Howard County Courthouse is not a good place to go if you're hungry. Smells of bacon, eggs, coffee, and other foods frequently fill the building, making many a stomach growl. This would be fine if the building contained a restaurant or cafeteria. It doesn't. The smells never have any source except for the "cooking ghost," one of several ghosts in the building.

Part of the Howard County Courthouse is Hayden House, also known as Oak Lawn. It once stood proudly on its own, but eventually the courthouse expanded until it enveloped it. Hayden House was a small stone house built in the 1800s by the first county clerk, Edwin Parson Hayden. He lived there until his death in 1850.

Hayden may still be roaming his old homestead. One morning a staff member saw a man through the window of the front door. But when she unlocked the door, no one was there. She searched the building, but found it empty. Others have seen a woman walk through the wall on the second floor. Another employee saw a white misty ball of vapor that hovered in midair on the stairway. Footsteps have also been heard in the building.

Numerous poltergeist-type activities have been experienced in the building. A coffee pot would heat up by itself, even after it was unplugged. Another worker had a hot plate that turned itself on several times. Even if she unplugged it, she would find the dial had been turned. A county employee working late in the building in 1974 reported hearing a rocking chair. The chair caused the floor boards to creak and the ceiling light to sway. Lights also turn themselves off and on.

OLD FIRE STATION
3829 Church Road, Ellicott City, 21043

The first fire chief in Elliott City was B. Harrison Shipley. He served from 1935 until 1957. Although he eventually retired, he continued to talk about his days with the fire department. He liked it so much, he decided to return after he passed away on September 26, 1967.

Shortly after Shipley's death, strange things began occurring at the firehouse. Firemen heard footsteps in unoccupied areas. Chairs moved by themselves. Doors slammed shut. Televisions turned on and off by themselves. Most believe it is Shipley's ghost, including his son, B. Harrison Shipley Jr., a retired fire administrator. In a 1997 *The Daily Grind* article, Shipley Jr. said, "That would be my father. Whenever things disappeared or the volunteers and paid firefighters heard odd noises, they'd blame it on 'Mr. Harry.' . . . Just recently he got blamed for a computer not working."

One Sunday afternoon the firehouse dog, Yogi, appeared to watch something come through the door and walk down the hall. Yogi immediately started after it and then began clawing and barking at one of the doors. The door was to an old apartment Shipley once lived in with his family. The firefighters opened the door, but no one was inside.

Although Shipley has never done anything malicious, it didn't stop the brave firefighters from being scared. Some would refuse to stay in the building alone.

PATAPSCO FEMALE INSTITUTE
3655 Church Road, Ellicott City, 21043

Katie was lost. Her parents had brought her to see the ruins of an old school and, after stopping to look at a butterfly, she had gotten separated from them and the rest of the group. Now she couldn't find them anywhere. As she walked to the front of the building, Katie saw a woman standing on the front steps. The woman lifted up the hem of her long gown and walked down the steps and across the front lawn. Hoping the woman would know where her group was, Katie rushed after her, only to watch her vanish in front of her eyes.

Katie had met Annie Van Derlot. According to legend Annie is a former student of the institute. Annie was the daughter of affluent Southerners. She was miserable at the school, especially during the long cold winter. Sadly, she contracted pneumonia and died her first year at the school. And although by all accounts she despised being at the school before her death, she does not seem to want to leave it after her death. Her ghost has been seen walking near the front of the school and is blamed for mysterious sounds coming from within the building.

However, research does not show any existence of Annie Van Derlot either at the school or anywhere else. Also, while the stories of Patapsco being haunted are widespread and well published, they are always nondescript. It's always "a young girl" or "people" who saw a ghostly lady, and nothing specific is ever documented. (For the record, Katie was not the young girl's real name but given here for the purposes of storytelling.)

Jacqueline Galke, executive director of the PFI told a newspaper in 2001, "The ghosts of the PFI are all fiction. I've never seen a ghost . . . I've been affiliated with PFI for about six years. I don't know anyone else here who's seen a ghost."

ST. MARY'S COLLEGE
4 ILCHESTER ROAD, ELLICOTT CITY, 21043

According to the legend of St. Mary's College, or Hell House, a priest sacrificed several students to the devil and arranged their bodies in a pentagram before committing suicide. Some versions replace the students with nuns. The deaths caused the school to close in the early 1970s. Now a deranged caretaker roams the property with his two rottweilers while carrying a loaded shotgun.

In truth, no students or nuns were ever murdered at St. Mary's. The school closed for the same reason many others do: lack of students. As to the deranged caretaker, well there is some truth to the story, but it's not a ghost story.

For many years, Allen Rufus Hudson was the property's caretaker. And he did have a reputation for chasing trespassers off with his dogs and his gun. He was even arrested for getting too ambitious in his protection of the property. He was arrested several times, including once in 1996 for shooting one trespasser. The charges were always dropped.

If Hudson seemed a little too aggressive, it wasn't enough to keep teens away. On Halloween night in 1997 a fire broke out in the seminary. By the time it was discovered the following morning, it was too late. The fire completely destroyed the five-story building. It also forced Hudson to move away from his home of twenty years, as the ruined building was in danger of falling on top of his home.

In 2006, the charred remains of St. Mary's were bulldozed. All that remains is a mysterious-looking stairway that leads to an altar and giant metal crucifix. This wasn't a satanic shrine, but the remains of a cemetery chapel.

SHORTER STORIES

The owner of **Bean Hollow**, a coffee shop, set up a surveillance camera in his shop after money went missing. She didn't catch a thief, but she did record people talking, whispers, scratches, and other sounds. "I was hearing all these voices and conversations and things going on, and there was no one in the store," Gretchen Shuey told the *Washington Post* in 2003. "It was random words and whispering." She also saw a menu fly out from under the cash register. Bean Hollow is located at 8059 Main Street.

The **B&O Railroad Museum**'s Ellicott City Station houses "Charlie," who likes to move boxes around and climb the stairs. On the plaza outside the museum, a member of a Civil War reenactor group decided to take a break and walked over to the old railroad bridge next to the museum. He noticed what appeared to be another reenactor who he hadn't seen before and immediately struck up a conversation with him. After a few moments the second man walked away from the area. When the man returned to his group for the reenactment, he was surprised the other man wasn't there. He asked around, but no one was missing and no one knew who the stranger was. The museum is located at 2711 Maryland Avenue.

At **Tea on the Tiber**, owners arrived to find paint splashed on the walls and floors during a renovation. They suspected vandals at first, but now believe it was the ghost of Kathryn, who hanged herself on the top floor. She also hides objects. The tea room is located at 8081 Main Street.

At **Wessel's Florist**, the ghost of a young boy moves items and leaves handprints. The flower shop is located at 8098 Main Street.

At **Su Casa**, the store's CD player turns off or switches songs when no one is touching it. They also found a box of lamps scattered across the store's floor. Manager Natalie Rinks reported seeing the apparition of a woman with long brown hair. Su Casa is located at 8307 Main Street.

At **Ellicott Mills Brewing Company**, the ghost of a man has been spotted. He is believed to be an accountant who was fired from a lumber store that occupied the building in the 1930s. He hung himself on the second floor of the building. Ellicott Mills Brewing Company is located at 8308 Main Street.

A new-age bookstore called the **Waning Moon** had trouble with books being tossed around the store at night. It was located at 3748 Old Columbia Pike. It has since closed. A jewelry store moved in, but has also closed.

Just down the road, at 3711 Old Columbia Pike, used to be **Al's Garage**. The owner, Al, died of a heart attack on the location. Since then the location has housed several different stores, and most of them have been haunted by Al. Al tickled the feet of yoga students and cast shadows when it was At The Well. When it was What's In Store, owner Chester Oderlock reported seeing a man standing below him when he was adjusting lights on the ladder. Startled, Oderlock screamed and the man disappeared. Oderlock saw Al several times after that and quickly learned to accept his presence. Today the location houses a beauty salon.

Chapter 11

Westminster

Westminster is even smaller than Ellicott City—only about nineteen hundred residents. Who knows what makes this small town so haunted, but it has a surprising number of ghost stories, including two headless ghosts and several irritable ones.

AVONDALE / LEGH FURNACE
507 STONE CHAPEL ROAD, WESTMINSTER, 21157

The legend of Legh (sometimes misspelled as Leigh) Master is one that should be told, but not necessarily believed. As is the case with a story that stretches back over two hundred years, the truth has been stretched with it.

Legh Master was born in London on May 5, 1717. Although he inherited quite a bit of property in England, he decided to sail to America in 1765 with his wife and daughter. He left his eleven-year-old son, Legh Hoskins Master, behind to serve as heir to his estate. He purchased property in Frederick County and started a smelting furnace.

During the Revolutionary War he operated a merchant boat in Bermuda, serving as transport to exchange prisoners between the British and Americans. It has been said he fled to Bermuda after his property was seized. His wife and daughter may have returned to England during this time. Either way, he returned to Legh Furnace after the war and continued to live there until his death in 1796. He was originally buried on the property, which was sold in 1802 to Isaac Van Bibber, who changed the name to Avondale, and the legend began.

In 1876 Van Bibber confessed the bones of Legh Master were no longer in his burial plot. He claimed years of bad weather had destroyed the tomb. On April 19, 1877, Master was buried in the graveyard of the Church of the Ascension in Westminster. Many believe it wasn't bad weather that brought Master's bones to the surface. No, he was so evil that the earth did not want to hold him. This seemed to be proven when the marble slab covering his new grave cracked.

According to legend, Master became infatuated with a female slave. She rejected his advances, but Master insisted. Another slave, named Sam, intervened on behalf of the young girl. Furious, Master pushed Sam into the furnace and burned him alive. He then walled the girl up either inside a wall in his house or inside the oven.

To add weight to the legend, people claim a skeleton was found in the oven when it was remodeled in 1930. Other stories say the body of a woman and child were found inside the wall of the kitchen in the house. Stories differ, either saying the bodies are Sam's wife and child or that they are a slave girl and a child she had with Master. No newspaper accounts of the supposed finding could be found to provide any weight to the stories.

Of course truth does not always have a place in ghostly legends, especially when so many claim to have had paranormal experiences attributed to the tale—like the sound of crying people hear coming from the house, even when it is empty. Or the upstairs door that refused to stay shut even after it was nailed closed. Then there was the man who noticed all the lights on inside the house shortly after Master died, even though no one was staying in the house. Tools hung neatly in the barn would be found scattered on the ground. The basement is also haunted by other slaves murdered by Master.

One of the scariest tales about Master is that he haunts the woods around his former home. People reported seeing him on a gray stallion snorting fire or on a horse's skeleton. Sometimes he was alone, other times he was pursued by three glowing imp-like characters. They said he was heard begging for mercy for his crimes and he was accompanied by the sound of rattling chains.

A ghostly black dog about three feet tall wearing a chain seen near Emmitsburg is said to be the ghost of Legh Master's dog. In 1887 two men riding near Ore Mine Bridge watched it walk through a fence, cross in front of them, and then walk through the fence on the other side of the road. One man tried to strike it with a whip, but the whip passed through it. Others have reported seeing the dog walk beside them before disappearing. No one seems to see the dog more than once.

CHRISTIAN ROYER HOUSE
817 FRIDINGER MILL ROAD, WESTMINSTER, 21157

The Fangmeyers knew living in a home built in the 1820s would be problematic, but some problems they could never have anticipated. Like when they found the TV and stereo turned on. They turned them off, only to watch them turn on again. Then there was the basement door that opened and closed on its own, usually when the family gathered together.

Of course, those things could be explained away as quirks of living in a two-hundred-year-old house. But the brown crayon marks that appeared on the freshly painted ceiling were not a quirk, and no one could explain how they got there.

When the dog started going into the guest room and barking at something, the husband thought they might have a rodent problem. But he never found any signs of mice or anything else to explain the dog's strange behavior. Then one night he came upstairs and heard something going on in the master bedroom. He was about to investigate, when the dog came barreling out of the adjoining room followed by a wicker basket sailing after the dog. Nothing was in the room that could have thrown the basket.

Other items were also moved around. Items on the coffee table were frequently moved during the night. During Christmas dinner, guests in the home observed a lit candle rise in the air, sail across the room, extinguish itself, and then fall to ground. During another gathering at Thanksgiving, a person thought a dog was tugging on his jacket until he turned to scold the dog and discovered the dog wasn't even in the room.

At least three ghosts have been connected to the house. One is a child who can be heard padding quickly down the hallway or playing with a ball. He is probably the one that enjoys removing cushions from the chairs and sofa and piling them on the floor. (Playing a ghostly game of "the floor is lava" perhaps?) He or she also has written the words "my love" in a childish script several times on a window screen.

Another ghost is a man in a Civil War uniform. He is seen sitting on the porch and rocking. He disappears whenever someone approaches. An unknown woman also has been seen in the house. People have also reported hearing voices talking and unexplained changes of temperature in the guest room. Today the house is a private residence. It was placed on the market and sold in June 2015.

COCKEY'S TAVERN
216 East Main Street, Westminster, 21157

The rumors of Cockey's Tavern being haunted have been around for a long time, not that everyone believes them. Although today it houses the Cockey's Exhibition Gallery, the Koontz-Yingling Learning Center, and The Shop at Cockey's Museum Store, it used to be a bar and restaurant. In 1981 two women came to Cockey's for lunch. One of them brought up the ghosts. The other one immediately said, "I don't believe in ghosts."

Suddenly she was struck on the head by a picture. The picture had fallen off the wall behind her. Oddly, the wire on the picture was not broken, and the nail it was on was still firmly in the wall. Even odder, the fall did not break the glass in the picture. The woman immediately told her friend, "I believe, I believe."

That wasn't the first or last time the ghost played with the pictures. On one occasion, staff arrived in the morning to find a picture of Grant that normally hung over the fireplace face down on one of the tables. Neither the picture nor the fine china place setting underneath were broken or even scratched. Later the staff was notified that one of the regulars, Mr. Walsh, had passed away. It was then they realized that the picture had been placed in Walsh's regular spot.

On another day, staff arrived to find a picture of a school teacher sitting on the floor. Neither the glass nor the hanging wire were damaged. Later they discovered that the teacher, who had once lived in the building, had passed away that morning.

The ghost, or rather ghosts, do more than move pictures. On one occasion after the staff had closed up and were getting ready to leave, they discovered that all of the candles on the mantel had been relit. The ghost would also rattle glasses and bottles in the bar.

Two different spirits have been seen in Cockey's. The first is a Civil War soldier. He is heard walking with heavy boots through the building and up the stairway. The second is a woman wearing a green colonial-style dress.

The Ghost of Cockey's Tavern is sometimes heard climbing the stairs at night. When shouted at to stop, the loud boot steps promptly cease. Until the restaurant closed, he was known to rattle the glasses and bottles in the bar when no one was around.

MCDANIEL COLLEGE
2 College Hill, Westminster, 21157

McDaniel College is a private, four-year college founded in 1867. The campus boasts about sixteen hundred students and at least three ghosts. The ghosts all live in Alumni Hall. Ironically, only one of the ghosts was ever a student at the college.

Harvey, a former student who loved the theater, died before graduating. One story says his parents were pressuring him to become a minister, but he wanted to go into theater. Unable to resolve the conflict, he committed suicide by jumping from the auditorium's balcony before graduation. Other people say he died after getting drunk and falling out of a window.

However he died, he likes to cause trouble. Superstition says that if his ghost is seen backstage before a production, good luck will follow. He is also blamed whenever things malfunction in the building. Lights flickering, unexplained sounds, and anything else that malfunctions is usually blamed on Harvey.

Dorothy Elderdice is the second ghost. Her picture hangs inside the Green Room. Her footsteps have been heard walking in the hallway just outside the room. Legend says that if a production is bad, her portrait will cry blood.

The last spirit is the most cantankerous, Mr. Steve. Mr. Steve used to run the costume shop, and he's still diligently doing his job. He's been known to steel scissors and measuring tapes. He gets unhappy when students make a mess and will rattle the cages that contain the costumes.

OLD OPERA HOUSE
140 East Main Street, Westminster, 21157

The line between comedy and insulting is a fine one—and one that Marshall Buell crossed during the Civil War. He performed at the Westminster's Opera House. Everything was going smoothly until he did his impression of Ulysses S. Grant and other government officials. Some of the audience took offense. A rock flew through the air onto the stage. Then another one, this time striking Buell in the neck. Buell quickly wrapped up his act and exited stage right.

The sheriff offered him protection for the night, but Buell needed to go to Hagerstown for his next performance. He was saddling his horse behind the building when he was attacked. His body was discovered with his throat slashed ear to ear.

A short time later, the town drunk reported seeing a man behind the Opera House gesturing wildly and talking as if doing a monologue, except no sound was coming out of his mouth. Everyone believed he was too far into his drink, until other people reported seeing the same thing. Some claim to have seen a headless ghost on the outside back stairs of the building.

Although the story sounds good, no documentation proving that Buell or anyone else was murdered at the Opera House exists. Nor is there any evidence that a performer named Marshall Buell existed at all. The Old Opera House is sometimes referred to at the Odd Fellow's Hall, as it also served that purpose in the past. Today it houses a printing company. Employees do report strange things happening, but nothing that they are willing to say on the record.

OLD JAIL
North Court Street, Westminster, 21157

Another headless ghost has been seen on North Court Street. It wanders about with his hands outstretched as if trying to find what he lost. The ghost belongs to Tom Parkes. In 1844 Parkes was sitting in the old jail. It was Christmas Eve, a depressing time to be in jail. He had been arrested for disturbing the peace and had put up a struggle. As he was a large man, the sheriff worried if it was wise to keep "Big Tom" or if it would be better to send him to Baltimore.

Parkes overheard the sheriff and became even more distraught. That night, he committed suicide by slicing his own throat. Dr. Zollickhoffer was summoned. Zollickhoffer was studying phrenology and felt Parkes was a prime specimen to study. He asked, and was granted, the man's head. The act dismayed Parkes so much that his ghost has returned, constantly searching for the head Zollickhoffer has taken.

THE KIMMEY HOUSE
201 East Main Street, Westminster, 21157

Before you complain about the long wait to see your doctor, talk to the ghost at the Kimmey House. He's been waiting to see Dr. George Colgate for close to two hundred years. Colgate used the house as an office back in the early 1800s. Today the house is owned and occupied by the Carroll County Historical Society.

Another Carroll County Historical Society house, the **Sherman-Fisher-Shellman House**, is also haunted. People report seeing a young girl in a white dress peering out at them from the windows when no one is in the house.

Chapter 12
Other Central

Elsewhere in the region is the Hampton Mansion. Now a historic site, it is has long history of being haunted, no matter how much the National Park Service likes to deny it. A couple of abandoned hospitals also exist here, and everyone knows those places are always haunted.

HAMPTON NATIONAL HISTORIC SITE
535 HAMPTON LANE, TOWSON, 21286

If you ask employees of the National Park Service if Hampton Mansion is haunted, they will insist that there are no ghosts there. They have been saying this for a number of years, but to date they have not been able to convince the ghosts.

Hampton Mansion was originally built by the Ridgely family in the early 1700s. It stayed in the family for two centuries, picking up a few ghosts as it passed from one generation to another. One famous legend about the mansion involves the daughter of Governor Thomas Swann, a friend of the Ridgelys. One of his daughters was ill and sent to the estate to recover. Eliza Ridgely, mistress of Hampton Mansion, was quite fond of the child and nicknamed her "Cygnet" or "Little Swan." One morning Cygnet came to the breakfast table complaining about a nightmare where a robed figure carrying a scythe chased her. Eliza brushed it off as simply a bad dream.

That night, a special ball had been prepared in Cygnet's honor. But when the time came, she failed to make an appearance. Finally a servant was sent to check on her. She was found slumped over at her dressing table dead. Since then people report seeing Cygnet Swann seated where she died in a northwest bedroom. She is described as dressed in her ball gown combing her blonde hair.

One problem with the story is the facts don't fit. Thomas Swann had five children, one boy and four girls. All four girls lived until adulthood and were married. There is no record of any of his children dying as a teenager. So the ghost may not be the daughter of Thomas Swann.

The mansion's second mistress, Priscilla Ridgely, is also believed to haunt the building, which seems odd since history suggests she was never happy there. The mansion was built between 1783 and 1790 by Captain Charles Ridgely. After his death, the mansion was inherited by Priscilla's husband, also named Charles.

While Charles was involved in politics and entertaining, Priscilla spent her time reading her bible and caring for the couple's thirteen children. She died when she was only fifty-two years old. She roams the mansion wearing a long gray gown. People report hearing the gown sweeping across the wood floors.

Priscilla is joined by Tom, a former butler who passed away in the late 1800s. He's been known to greet people at the door. On one occasion, he gave a guest a tour of the house before disappearing.

Probably the most trustworthy ghost stories are found in *A Park Ranger's Life: Thirty-two Years Protecting Our National*

Parks by Bruce Bytnar. Bytnar was often called to investigate incidents at Hampton in the 1970s and even spent two weeks in the house during an exhibition of needlework.

Bytnar tells about a meeting in the basement conference room that was disrupted by continual tapping on the floor above them. Finally they sent someone to figure out the cause of the tapping and get it to stop. On his way up the stairs, the man was greeted by someone meeting in the room above them who had come down to ask them to please stop tapping on the ceiling. Bytnar investigated the basement ceiling and there were no pipes, heating ducts, or anything else that might have caused the tapping.

The shutters on the house were another continual problem. The shutters had been designed to be closed over the window as a measure or protection during storms. The National Park Service installed alarms in the house that included sensors on the shutters that would sound if someone opened them. In order to turn the alarm on, all the shutters had to be closed.

Yet, somehow, the shutters were found open in the morning, even though the alarm was set. The alarm company was called, but everything was working properly. There was no way anyone should have been able to set the alarm if the shutters were open or open the shutters once the alarm was set.

Bytnar had several unexplained experiences when he was required to spend several nights in the house. He heard footsteps walking on the third floor, found objects moved when no one had been in the room, and heard a broken clock chiming. The incidents continued until he loudly explained to the ghosts that he was only there for a few days to protect the house.

A famous story about Hampton involves the chandelier. Legend says that over the years residents have heard it crashing to the floor. The sound is so loud, that everyone in the mansion hears it. But when they investigate, the chandelier is still hanging where it normally is. It is believed that the event foretells tragedy at Hampton, and that in the past every time it's heard, the mistress of the house has died. However, there have been reports of people hearing the sound since the Park Service took it over, and no one has died afterward.

The chandelier is not the only ghostly sound here. People often hear the sound of a door opening or closing, but none of the doors are moved. Others have heard the sound of a harpsichord being played, even though there's never been one on the property.

But not all the incidents have been harmless. One of the ghosts didn't like the temporary displays set up in the great hall and continually knocked them over. Eventually staff decided not to use that room for displays anymore. It wasn't worth the effort.

Hampton Mansion remained in the Ridgely family until 1947, when it was donated to the National Park Service. They have restored the house and provide tours through the house and around the grounds. Sadly, no ghost tours are offered.

ROSEWOOD CENTER
ROSEWOOD LANE AND AXIS ROAD, OWINGS MILLS, 21117

All abandoned insane asylums must be haunted, even if they are not. Rosewood Center was established in 1888 as the Asylum and Training School for the Feeble Minded. Like many facilities of this era, patient neglect abuse was a major problem. It wasn't until 1981 that the US Justice Department recognized that patients "failed to receive minimally adequate care." Additional investigations caused several of the older buildings to be condemned in 1989. Then in 2006, the main building was burned due to arson. Another building fell victim to arson in 2009. Later that same year, Rosewood was closed.

Reports of ghosts at Rosewood are vague. The only specific account is seeing a woman standing in a window of the third floor of the main building. This building has been fenced off since the 2006 fire. Ghost hunters who consider visiting Rosewood should keep in mind that the property is protected by security guards. Not to mention the ground has high levels of arsenic in it, and the buildings are filled with asbestos and lead paint.

HENRYTON HOSPITAL
7910 HENRYTON CENTER ROAD, MARRIOTTSVILLE, 21104

Henryton Hospital suffers a fate similar to Rosewood Center. It's an abandoned hospital that everyone claims is haunted. It was closed in 1985. Since then it has been plagued by vandalism and fires. No substantial evidence or stories exist to suggest the ghost stories connected to it are true. It was recently slated for demolition and may no longer exist.

GEORGE FOX MIDDLE SCHOOL
7922 OUTING AVENUE, PASADENA, 21122

The legends surrounding George Fox Middle School are a perfect example of how stories get stretched. People say the ghost of the first principal walks the corridors of the school. She was an unpleasant woman and very strict. Sometimes her ghost is seen pulling a student down the corridor by his ear. They say she likes to haunt the sixth-grade hallway, gym locker rooms, and boiler room. Accounts from students of the school tell how they were told by relatives that the principal died during the school year of a "mysterious cause" and that she is buried under the building.

The first principal of the school was Mary Farrell. She was principal from 1949 until 1974, when she retired. She also seems to have been well liked. The 1951 yearbook was dedicated to her and reads in part, "Her never-ending work, patience and cooperation in organizing and improving our school through the two years of its existence will never be forgotten. We are proud to have such a wonderful person helping us . . ." There is also a scholarship in her name created by one of her former students.

Farrell died six months after retiring in 1974. And although where she is buried is not clear, it is highly unlikely she would have been buried under the school.

Part 4

CAPITAL

The Capital Region consists of the counties that wrap around Washington DC: Frederick, Prince George's, and Montgomery. It is the most densely populated area of the state. Located farther north, Frederick County has a more rural feel to it than Prince George's and Montgomery Counties, which immediately border the nation's capital. This is also home to Burkittsville, which was made famous in *The Blair Witch Project*. The stories told in the film are pure fiction and most of the movie wasn't even shot in the town, but rather in nearby Montgomery County.

Chapter 13
Civil War Battlefields

Frederick County was the site of two separate Civil War battles. The first was the Battle of South Mountain on September 14, 1862. South Mountain involved three separate battles for passes through the mountains: Crampton's, Turner's, and Fox's Gap. The second was the Battle of Monocacy on July 9, 1864. It is called the "Battle that saved Washington" because it delayed a Confederate attack on Washington DC by one day. The delay allowed Union reinforcements to get in place and protect the capital. While these were not major battles of the war, they did create a few ghosts.

WISE FARM
21605 RENO MOUNTAIN ROAD, BOONSBORO, 21713

On approximately September 17, 1862, Daniel Wise returned to his farm to find it littered with bodies. The Fox's Gap portion of the Battle of South Mountain occurred three days earlier, and Wise's farm had been in the midst of it. South Mountain wasn't the bloodiest or most important battle of the Civil War. It had "only" five thousand casualties, which doesn't even put it the top 10 bloodiest battles of the war.

South Mountain is the name given the northern ridge of the Blue Ridge Mountains that divides Hagerstown Valley and Cumberland Valley from eastern Maryland. There are only a handful of areas where the mountains can be crossed. On September 14, 1862, the forces of Major General George McClellan and General Robert E. Lee fought at three of them. McClellan had learned that Lee had divided his forces. McClellan hoped to attack him while he was vulnerable. But first he had to get through one of three passes: Crampton's, Turner's, or Fox's Gap.

Having learned of McClellan's plan, Lee sent forces to each one. Battles waged throughout the day at all three. By dusk Union forces managed to take Crampton's Gap, and Lee ordered his troops to withdraw. Although he lost the battle, he delayed McClellan enough that he was able to reunite his army before had had to face McClellan again. The two met in battle three days later at Antietam.

According to legend, the army offered Wise five dollars to bury the bodies on his farm. Rather than go to the work of digging individual graves, he threw them into a half-dug well on the farm and covered them with dirt. But Wise didn't enjoy the fortune for long. As he was sitting on his porch, he saw a figure coming down the lane. He soon recognized it as a Confederate soldier, but to Wise's horror he discovered he could see through the man.

"Turn me over!" the ghost moaned.

"What?" Wise asked.

"I'm most uncomfortable lying on my face. Turn me over! Please!" the ghost said again before disappearing from sight.

Whether it was guilt or fear is unclear, but Wise immediately set to rectifying the problem. He dug up the well and pulled the bodies out. Sure enough, as he pulled the bodies out he discovered one that looked exactly like the specter . . . of course, he didn't realize it until he turned the body over, as it was facing down in the well.

As frightening as this story is, it seems to be a work of fiction. The Wise farm was in the center of the skirmish at Fox's Gap and served as a field hospital according to paperwork on file with the Maryland Historical Trust. The document also mentions the land was used as a burial ground afterward and that "The Confederate bodies were disinterred in 1874 from the well where they had been deposited." It doesn't mention who originally put the bodies in the well.

According to several sources, Wise returned to his farm and found his well ruined. He asked for one dollar per body in the well and was given sixty dollars. Other sources dispute this version of the story. Either way, the bodies were placed in the well, although they didn't remain there.

In 1874 Henry C. Mumma was paid $1.65 for each body he exhumed from the well and properly buried at the Washington Confederate Cemetery in Hagerstown. By this point they were nothing but bones. Fifty-eight bodies were taken from the well.

Today, Wise's farm is gone. According to maps it was located on what is now Reno Monument Road where the Appalachian Trail intersects it. It is also close to monuments to Brigadier General Samuel Garland Jr. and Major General Jesse Lee Reno, both of whom died at Fox's Gap.

In 2003 a new monument was erected about a thousand feet south of the Garland and Reno monuments in honor of North Carolinians who fought at or near the location. It reads, in part, "Two days after the battle, 58 Confederate dead were dumped down the well of Daniel Wise located NW."

An interesting footnote: Two future presidents fought at Fox's Gap: Rutherford B. Hayes and William McKinley. Hayes received a serious wound at Fox's Gap. McKinley wasn't wounded, but died thirty-nine years to the day of the battle after being shot by an assassin's bullet.

GATHLAND STATE PARK
900 Arnoldstown Road, Jefferson, 21755

Gathland State Park is located on land originally owned by George Townsend. Townsend was a journalist who used the pen name "Gath." During the Civil War, he worked as a war correspondent. Later, in 1884, he bought land on South Mountain. Immediately he started building his estate, called Gapland. While Gapland had the usual things found on an estate, like a home and servant's quarters, it also included a few unique things—like the War Correspondents Memorial Arch, the first monument dedicated to journalists killed in combat. Townsend completed it in 1896. He also had a tomb constructed where he intended to be buried, allowing him to spend eternity on his beloved estate.

Unfortunately Townsend abandoned Gapland in 1906 after his wife died. He died penniless in 1914 in New York City and was buried next to his wife in Philadelphia. However, he hasn't given up his dream of spending eternity on his estate. People have reported hearing footsteps around his former home.

His ghost is not alone. Townsend purposefully bought land where the Battle of Crampton's Gap was fought. And like most of the Civil War battlefields, the site is haunted. People report seeing Civil War soldiers in the woods along with phantom campfires. Cannon fire has also been heard.

UNION CEMETERY

BURKITTSVILLE ROAD AND CEMETERY DRIVE, BURKITTSVILLE, 21718

Anyone who has seen *The Blair Witch Project* will recognize this cemetery from the beginning of the film. But the ghosts here were not even mentioned in the film. After the Battle for Crampton's Gap, citizens brought the bodies of both Union and Confederate soldiers and buried them in shallow graves. They assumed that the armies would return for their dead. They did, eventually. It wasn't until 1868 that the bodies were exhumed and moved to other cemeteries including Washington Confederate Cemetery. People report seeing strange lights and soldiers wandering around the cemetery grounds.

MONOCACY NATIONAL BATTLEFIELD

5201 URBANA PIKE, FREDERICK, 21704

In 1993, members of the Maryland TriState Paranormal were investigating Monocacy Battlefield. One of the members reported seeing what appeared to be a ghostly encampment on the battlefield. As he was pointing to the area where he claimed to see the encampment, another member took his picture. Next to the man was a gray-colored mass.

According to Jack Farrell in his book *Mystical Experiences*, photographers consider Monocacy "among the most ghost-laden." Photographer Tracy Manseau told Farrell that photographs she takes there frequently contain orbs or balls of light.

The Battle of Monocacy was fought on July 9, 1864, when Lieutenant General Jubal Early and Major General Lew Wallace faced off. Early managed to lead his Confederate forces and defeat Wallace, but the battle ended up being a win for the Union. Early's march toward Washington DC was delayed by one day, giving the Union time to strengthen the troops around the capital. The Confederates still launched an attack on July 12, but were forced to retreat into Virginia.

But you don't have to have a camera to have an experience here. Photographer C. R. Angleberger was camping on the battlefield. In the middle of the night, he heard several voices walking by his tent that sounded to him like soldiers.

Another visitor watched what she thought was a group of five Union soldiers walking on the battlefield. It wasn't until the men walked through a fence as if it wasn't there that she realized they were ghosts.

A motorcyclist riding through the park stopped to adjust something on his bike. He noticed what appeared to be a farmer walking through the field carrying a rake. As the farmer got closer, the motorcyclist realized that the man was dressed like a Confederate soldier and the object he was carrying was actually a musket.

Chapter 14

Frederick

The city of Frederick became a major crossroad during the Civil War. Armies passed through here on their way to Antietam and Gettysburg. It is also close to the Battles of South Mountain and Monocacy. As a result, Frederick had several hospitals during the war. To find out more, check out the National Museum of Civil War Medicine, which has its own ghosts. But not all the ghosts here are connected to the Civil War. Frederick City Hall is haunted by a ghost of a man who was executed in a brutal manner, while the Frederick Historical Society and the Weinberg Center for the Arts are both haunted by former employees.

NATIONAL MUSEUM OF CIVIL WAR MEDICINE
48 EAST PATRICK STREET, FREDERICK, 21705

George Wunderlich often hears footsteps walking about eight to ten feet behind him when he arrives in the morning. But he's learned not to check to see who is behind him, because no one would be there. Or no one living, at least, or that he could see.

Disembodied footsteps are just one of many paranormal things Wunderlich has experienced as the executive director of the National Museum of Civil War Medicine. In a 2010 interview for the *Frederick News-Post*, he talked about some of the other experiences he has heard about.

"Recently several of my employees commented to one of my coworkers, Nicky, that they had seen a man walk into her office and turn off the light. Well there's only one way in and out of her office and they never saw anyone reappear and there was no one in there."

But it wasn't their eyes playing tricks on them. According to Wunderlich, "We've had at least two instances where figures have appeared on our surveillance cameras and disappeared in that very same area. It appears to be a gentleman in light-colored clothing with a light-colored hat on his head."

As if that wasn't enough, sometimes the ghosts like to reach out and touch. On one occasion, a curator was in the collection room talking about ghosts with his wife.

"I don't believe in that stuff," his wife told him. As soon as she spoke, she felt a push on her shoulder. Thinking her husband was joking around with her, she turned to look at him, only to find him standing across the room and no one else standing near her. Visitors to the museum have also reported feeling someone brush up against them when no one else was close to them. The sound of children playing or giggling is also commonly heard in the museum, even when no children are present.

Working late at night at the museum is always an adventure for employees, especially when they work alone. April Dietrich recounted some things that happened to her in a 2014 article published on Your4State.com.

"All of a sudden I'd be working, typing away, and there it would go, the paper clips would just fly across the room. We have doors opening and closing, people walking up and down the halls," Dietrich said. "I can hear conversations. I hear computer noises, everything that would sound like a regular day at the office I can hear at night."

The museum was once owned by James Whitehill before he sold it to Clarence Carty after the Civil War. Both men used the building as a combination furniture store and embalming center. (Servicing people in every stage of their life it seems.) During the Civil War, it is believed as many as ten thousand bodies were embalmed there. That shouldn't be too surprising considering Frederick is close to five major Civil War Battlefields: Gettysburg, Harpers Ferry, Antietam, South Mountain, and Monocacy.

Wunderlich is not the only one to have an early morning paranormal experience. Karen Thomassen, former deputy director at the museum, heard a doorbell go off behind her one morning at seven. According to Thomassen, she was alone in the building when she heard it, but that is not the only reason why she knew somebody hadn't rung the bell, because the bell isn't connected to anything. In other words, it cannot go off at all.

Although Wunderlich claims the spirits are not malevolent, at least one unnamed curator might disagree with him. She had climbed a ladder to change a lightbulb when the ladder was knocked out from underneath her. She was able to grab a ceiling pipe to keep from falling and breaking her neck.

But in general the ghosts behave themselves well according to Dietrich. "If they start making too much noise, you tell them to calm it down, and they usually do." That's something that can't be said about some of the patrons to the museum.

SCHIFFERSTADT ARCHITECTURAL MUSEUM
1110 ROSEMONT AVENUE, FREDERICK, 21701

The office of the Schifferstadt Architectural Museum is on the second floor. To get to it, one must go through the main door into the gift shop, and then open a second door to a stairway going upstairs. To prevent unauthorized guests from traversing upstairs, someone hung a set of bells on the door to alert employees whenever the door was opened.

Amelia Cotter, an intern at the Schifferstadt Architectural Museum, was working alone in the office on the second floor when she heard the door opening, the bells jingle, and then heavy footsteps on the stairs. "I figured someone was coming up and I just hadn't heard the main front door open," Cotter wrote in her book *Maryland Ghosts: Paranormal Encounters in the Free State.*

"At some point, they just stopped. I stopped typing and looked up, wondering why the person wasn't saying anything and had stopped halfway up the stairs. I had the distinct impression that there was a man there, and got up from my desk to walk over and see who he was. Of course, I saw no one, and the gift shop door was still closed." Weirded out, but not frightened, Cotter returned to her desk and continued working.

A number of people have heard disembodied footsteps walking through Schifferstadt. Most believe ghosts of Joseph and Elias Bruner haunt the location. Joseph Bruner emigrated from Germany in the 1700s. He purchased the land and built a modest house in 1746. Joseph sold the property to his youngest son, Elias Bruner, in 1753. Five years later Elias built the stone house that stands today, although both the interior and exterior have been altered a number of times through the years.

In 2010, Mason-Dixon Paranormal Society (MDPS) investigated the house and caught a number of EVP, including some of which sounded like German.

According to Darryl Keller, one of the founders of MDPS, the cellar of the house is one of the most active locations in the house. During the investigation all of the investigators experienced the feeling of being touched or lightly pushed.

"If you go in [the cellar], especially down in the basement with the lights out and just start asking questions, within 30 minutes if you don't feel something brush up against you or just slightly push you, I would be truly amazed," he told the *Frederick News-Post*.

Two other ghosts believed to haunt the Schifferstadt include a woman and young boy. The female spirit is found in the kitchen area. Michael J. and Michael H. Varhola give the name "Wilhelmina" to the spirit in their book *Ghosthunting Maryland*. They claim Wilhelmina was a midwife who died after her clothing caught fire. She is known to be a kind ghost who often strokes peoples' cheeks and has even hugged them.

"Isaiah" is the name given to the little boy who haunts the office. The name came after several neighbors stopped by to set up a playdate with Isaiah after he played with their child. The neighbors were shocked to discover that no child named Isaiah had been staying at the house. Visitors to the museum have reported seeing the figure of a little boy in one of the corners of the attic.

Other phenomena reported at Schifferstadt include hearing doors slam and the sounds of hammering and other construction-like sounds.

BARBARA FRITCHIE HOUSE
154 West Patrick Street, Frederick, 21701

The Barbara Fritchie House proves a person doesn't have to live in a house in order to haunt it. Tour guides report seeing a rocking chair moving on its own and an indentation on the bed as if someone is sitting there. One guide even reported seeing a pair of feet sticking out from underneath the quilt.

They believe the ghost is Barbara Fritchie, although it is a 1927 re-creation of her original house. The original house was damaged in a flood and then torn down, according to newspaper articles published in 1869 and 1875, because it was in the way of a bridge being constructed (or widened) across Carroll Creek.

In 1927 her house was reconstructed at 154 West Patrick Street. The new house is smaller and situated differently because of modifications to the banks of Carroll Creek.

Fritchie became famous after John Greenleaf Whittier wrote a poem about her in 1863. According to the poem, the elderly woman bravely waved the Union flag from her attic window in front of Confederate troops led by Stonewall Jackson daring the rebel troops to fire on her. The poem was written two years after Fritchie died at the age of ninety-five.

It wasn't long after the poem was published before people questioned the historical accuracy of the poem. In reality, Fritchie was sick in bed when the Confederate troops marched through the town on their way to Antietam. She had ordered her flag to be taken down, but the servants failed to do so, resulting in the flag being a favorite target of the troops as they passed through. A woman did bravely wave the Union flag that day, but it was Fritchie's neighbor, Mary Quantrell.

According to most of the stories published about the haunting, the basement lights in the house next door turn on and off. The stories attribute this to Fritchie's ghost because she "also occupied" it. Although, since she never occupied the house that bears her name, but still haunts it, it doesn't seem she needs to reside in a house in order to haunt it.

FREDERICK CITY HALL
101 NORTH COURT STREET, FREDERICK, 21701

Peter Sueman (sometimes spelled Suman or Sutman) has every reason to be upset, considering how he was treated before he died. On August 17, 1791, he was the first of three men to be executed for high treason. Sueman and six other men were found guilty for having recruited and sworn in troops to fight for England. He might be angry because he was falsely convicted (as some suggest) or over the way he was killed.

Judge Hanson issued the following sentence: "You will be carried to the gaol of Fredrick County and thence be drawn to the gallows of Frederick-Town and be hanged theron; you shall be cut down to the earth alive, and your entrails shall be taken out, and burnt while you are yet alive; your head shall be cut off; your body shall be divided into four parts, and your head and quarters shall be placed where his Excellence the Governor shall appoint—So Lord have mercy upon your poor souls!"

To be fair to the judge, he wasn't being creative or overly aggressive; it was the listed punishment for treason at the time. And the sentence was carried out as prescribed, but only to Sueman. After his execution, the crowd was so horrified by what they had witnessed, they begged for mercy for the remaining men. Two men were simply hanged, the other four were pardoned by the governor. (Interestingly, one of the two men hanged was John Fritchie, Barbara Fritchie's father-in-law.)

According to legend, Sueman cursed the courthouse building before (or during) his execution, which could explain why the courthouse burned down shortly after his execution. A second building was built in the same spot, only to burn down in 1861. According to reports at the time, the fire started in several spots at the same time and when the fire brigade arrived, the water supply had been mysteriously turned off.

The new building is not without problems. Thumps and clangs are heard at night, toilets flush on their own, faucets and lights turn on and off by themselves, calendars switch months ahead, and pictures on the wall become slanted overnight. The elevator has also been known to operate on its own, opening at floors with no one inside.

According to Judy Arnold, the city's facility manager, in a 2010 article for the *Frederick News-Post*, the radio in her second floor office turned on one day when she was working. "I didn't have it on. It just started playing."

A shadowy figure dressed in black Victorian clothing has also been seen in the building, but some don't believe this is Sueman's ghost, but that of his widow. After her husband's death, she gathered his body and buried it. Afterward, she was often seen standing over his grave to protect it.

HISTORICAL SOCIETY OF FREDERICK COUNTY
24 EAST CHURCH STREET, FREDERICK, 21701

An employee was working late at the Historical Society of Frederick County when she heard music coming from one of the rooms. When she paused to listen, she noticed the music sounded grainy as if coming from an old record player, like the Grafonola phonograph. But the Grafonola phonograph was broken, and even if it worked, it would require someone to crank it and no one else was in the building.

Hearing the Grafonola is one of many odd things that happen at the historical society. It is located in the former home of John Loats. He built the house in 1835. When he died in 1879, it became the Loats Female Orphans Asylum, which continued until 1958. After it closed, a legal battle began between the city of Frederick and heirs of Loats over the property. Once it was settled (in favor of the city), the city sold it to the historical society.

Although the name suggests a dark place, Loats Female Orphans Asylum was by all accounts a positive place. The staff was dedicated and the girls happy and well cared for. It seems someone from that time was so happy there they decided to stay. Forever.

The ghost has been seen on several occasions. She is described as pale and wearing an old-fashioned white dress with a high collar and long sleeves. Her hair is pulled up into a bun. Her spirit has been seen walking in the corridors and sitting in an old antique rocking chair. When not listening to music or roaming the house, she moves trunks around. Staff continually find trunks moved from one area of the house to another.

LANDON HOUSE
3401 Urbana Pike, Frederick, 21704

In 2003 a worker at Landon House watched as a man dressed in a Civil War uniform walked in the front door. Knowing no reenactments were scheduled, the worker stood up to ask the man why he was there. The soldier paused briefly in the foyer, then continued up the staircase before disappearing into thin air.

The Landon House was intended to be a silk mill along the Rappahannock River in Virginia. When things changed, the building was moved by barge to Frederick in 1840. At first it was the Shirley Female Academy and then the Landon Military Academy and Institute.

During the first Maryland campaign of the Civil War, Landon served as the headquarters for General J. E. B. "Jeb" Stuart. Stuart was not one to let war interfere (too much) with his social life. He held a number of social events including the Sabers and Roses Ball, a soiree for rebel troops, on September 8, 1862. During the ball he received a report that Union cavalry were in Hyattstown and headed toward Urbana. Stuart paused the festivities and he and his men headed out. He arrived to discover the Union soldiers had already been repulsed, so they returned to Landon House and continued the ball.

Ten days later, the men would fight the Battle of Antietam, the bloodiest day of the Civil War. Landon House, like many other properties, was transformed into a military hospital. Whether it is the soldiers who danced or the ones who died here is unclear.

In 2005, construction workers working behind the property approached Ken Dolan, who owned the property at the time, if a reenactment was being held that day. "I said no," Dolan told a reporter for Gazette.net, "and they told me that a guy dressed in a Union uniform came out of the woods, waved to them and then disappeared back into the woods."

The basement—like all basements—tends to be creepy and believed by some to be the most haunted area. Urban legends about Landon House state it used to house slaves or the hounds used to chase down slaves. According to one legend, during the Civil War dogs were left in the basement and starved to death. However, the scratches are more likely from dogs kept by previous owners of the house after the Civil War, when the property became a private home. Scratches on the wall from said dogs can still be seen, and ghostly howling, barking, and scratching are often heard.

But the basement dogs are not the only spectral animal at Landon House. Another dog is said to have come to the house after being wounded at the battle of Antietam. The dog died from his wounds and never left. A photographer once caught an image at Landon House that contained the image of a ghostly dog and woman.

Another ghostly woman commonly seen by children of the house roams the second floor of the house doing a bedtime check. She likely worked in the house when it was a female academy. A third woman is seen on the balcony of the house. Legend says she lost her baby during childbirth. She rocked the baby for three days before accepting its death.

Other paranormal phenomena that occur at Landon House include hearing Civil War music; feeling like you're being watched; unexplained cold spots, orbs, and mists; and seeing ghostly lights moving through the house.

WEINBERG CENTER FOR THE ARTS
20 West Patrick Street, Frederick, 21701

The Tivoli Theatre opened in 1926, which in Frederick means it isn't that old. But it was the largest building in town and one of the most opulent: uniformed ushers, crystal chandeliers, velvet chairs, and a Wurlitzer organ. Sadly, as years passed attendance at the theater declined—as did the theater's opulence. In 1976, Mother Nature delivered her a fatal blow by flooding the theater with water and mud.

The owners decided to donate the building to the city. Rather than tear it down, they restored the theater to its original glory. They might not have if they had known the building came with its own ghost. Little is known about "Jimmy" except that he was a projectionist at the Tivoli until he died of a heart attack. But being dead hasn't kept Jimmy from coming to work. Many people claim to have felt Jimmy's presence when in the theater, but that's not enough for him.

Jimmy gets upset when new employees start working at "his" theater and has been known to mess up the bathroom in retaliation. He also has vandalized the vending machines and caused power outages in the building. If you decide to take a job at the Weinberg, make sure to give Jimmy his deserved due. According to one employee, he called out, "Goodnight, Jimmy!" before leaving, and ever since then the ghost has left him alone.

MARYLAND SCHOOL FOR THE DEAF
101 CLARKE PLACE, FREDERICK, 21701

Strange figures can be seen peering out the windows and voices are often heard in one building at the Maryland School for the Deaf. It used to be a former Hessian barracks and dates back to the French and Indian War. It was used in other wars, too, including the Revolutionary War to house troops by General Edward Braddock, as a prison after the war, and as a makeshift hospital during the Civil War. Many believe the figures are either soldiers who died during a fire in the building or Civil War soldiers who died there.

TYLER-SPITE HOUSE
112 WEST CHURCH STREET, FREDERICK, 21701

Tyler-Spite House got its name after Dr. John Tyler built it to prevent a road from being built across his land. In 1814 a crew arrived at the site to discover a newly poured foundation for the house and Dr. Tyler sitting in a rocking chair on top. He had a crew pour it the night before.

So given Tyler's nature, it shouldn't surprise anyone that he's made his displeasure known. His spirit remained at rest until someone transformed his house into apartments. Suddenly the property was plagued with odd noises, unseen touches, and the usual variety of ghostly phenomena.

Artist Maria Theresa Fernandes reported waking in a cold sweat at 2:30 a.m. every night she stayed at the house. She would then hear heavy footsteps on the attic stairs, and a white haze would appear. The haze would eventually form a gaunt man with long stringy hair. He would stand next to her and poke her in the ribs with his bony fingers.

GASLIGHT ANTIQUES
118 EAST CHURCH STREET, FREDERICK, 21701

Residents at the house on Church Street have pots and pans move around and often hear loud crashes. They believe it is their resident ghost venting her frustration. According to urban legend, a woman in her forties gave birth when the building was a boardinghouse. But after the baby died, the despondent woman hanged herself from the balcony (which may be why residents have reported hearing a baby crying, even though no baby was around). Other people have reported having their covers pulled off their bed and seeing a dark figure resembling a woman in the house. The location used to be a store called Gaslight Antiques, but it is now a private residence.

ROGER BROOKE TANEY HOUSE
121 SOUTH BENTZ STREET, FREDERICK, 21701

People report seeing Robert Brooke Taney walking around the grounds of his namesake house. However, it is unlikely that it is Taney's ghost they are seeing (if it is a ghost at all). Taney never lived there. He owned the property, but that is all. According to the Historical Society of Frederick County, the house *"interprets* the life of Taney and his wife Anne Key (sister of Francis Scott Key), as well as various aspects of life in early nineteenth century Frederick." So maybe what people are seeing is just a ghostly interpretation of Taney?

Chapter 15
Capital Education

When looking for an afterlife education, the Capital Region of Maryland must be where you go. Three colleges and a high school all have several ghosts. Even more surprising is that all four schools admit that they have ghosts. Usually, schools tend to deny them.

MOUNT SAINT MARY'S UNIVERSITY
1630 OLD EMMITSBURG ROAD, EMMITSBURG, 21727

A severed hand, a ghostly nun, a Civil War soldier, and a poltergeist priest all wander the haunted grounds of Mount Saint Mary's University. Apparently ghosts come here to receive an education. Which makes sense since it is the second-oldest Catholic institution in the country. (Georgetown University is the oldest.)

The creepiest tale at the university is of a slave named Leander. He lived on the first floor of what is now McCaffrey Hall (some legends say his former slave quarters were once located here). He was accused of stealing and his left hand was cut off. The hand was buried in the quadrangle. Leander continued working at the college, even after gaining his freedom, and is buried in the school's cemetery. Leander moved on, but his hand hasn't found peace yet.

Residents of McCaffrey Hall keep their windows closed and locked at night unless they want to find Leander's hand crawling inside in search of its missing body. Students have also reported seeing the hand wandering the campus and have heard it scratching at windows.

Other students have reported seeing a ghostly nun walking the hallways of the school. She is believed to be Elizabeth Ann Seton. Seton arrived in 1809 and established a parochial school for girls in Emmitsburg that later became Saint Joseph's College. Saint Joseph's closed in 1973 and sent its students to Mount Saint Mary's, which became coeducational.

Seton's ghost is usually accompanied by a man with a doctor's bag. Two different theories exist on the identity of the doctor. Saint Joseph's was used as a hospital during the Civil War. Although Seton died in 1821, wounded soldiers reported seeing a vision of a nun during their time here. Perhaps a Civil War doctor decided to join Seton in her ghostly rounds. It could also be her father, who was a physician.

The ghostly duo visit frequently enough that the university has acknowledged the sightings. According to Linda Sherman, a university spokeswoman, "Occasionally, I think she's guiding us. If not her ghost, then it's her persona."

Another religious specter at Mount Saint Mary's is Reverend Simon Brute, a former president who died on campus in 1839. He walks around campus wearing long black robes. People who see him report he usually smiles at them, nods, and moves on.

The residential housing that bears Brute's name is also haunted, or at least one room is. The story can be traced back to a story told to Michael Norman and Beth Scott for their book *Haunted Heritage*. Father Daniel Nusbaum lived in the room for three years when he was a professor at the college. He had a number of experiences with the ghost. Things often moved around the room while he was sleeping.

"And these all were not events where I wondered if that's where I had put (the objects) the night before. It was obvious that they had been moved," Father Daniel claimed. For example the clock on a mantelpiece that moved from one end to the other, and then to the middle, then back to other end. Objects would fall off shelves and doors opened and closed on their own. But one of the oddest things happened with the bathroom.

"In the little hallway off the sitting room of this apartment there was a closet on one side and the bathroom on the other side. I'd wake up at night because the bathroom door squeaked. It would open and the light would go on and then the door would close. I always thought that was especially weird, because why would a ghost ever need a bathroom? Or need to turn on the light?"

Legend says that other priests who lived in that room had similar experiences. One priest had just finished cleaning his room before stepping out for a few minutes. When he returned, the room was in total disarray. His lights and television often turned themselves on and off.

In 1997 the room was transformed into student housing after many years of being vacant (by the living at least). Students who have had the privilege of living in that room report objects falling off the walls, the toilet flushing by itself, and the TV switching channels on its own.

Students also report seeing a ghost dressed as a Civil War soldier who taps them on the shoulder and begs them, "Turn me over." According to the story, he promised his beloved he'd think about her while away. The two looked up and agreed to look at the same star every night. He died at Gettysburg and was buried in an old well, face down. Unable to see the star, he is looking for someone to correct the error. (The story's similarity to Daniel Wise's story at South Mountain Battlefield, combined with a lack of details, suggests this story might be just a story. See chapter 13 for that story.)

HOOD COLLEGE
401 ROSEMOUNT AVENUE, FREDERICK, 21701

Amanda S. was leaving Brodbeck Music Hall when she experienced something she couldn't explain. "My friend and I were getting ready to leave when she heard piano music coming from the stage," she told the campus newspaper, *The Blue and Gray.* "So I followed her up there, and I felt this presence behind the piano. When I looked I saw a blue silhouette. I felt threatened, so we left."

Staff and other students also have reported hearing music coming from the stage area when no one else is in the building. Orbs are also commonly seen floating down from the balcony to the stage.

A security guard was locking the doors when he heard footsteps from the stage area. His routine was to lock the first door, walk through the building, then lock the other doors on his way out. When he heard footsteps, he immediately called out to see if someone was still in the building. No one answered. But he continued to hear footsteps walking across the empty stage. After that night he started locking all the doors from the outside.

The third floor, which is off-limits due to safety reasons, is supposed to be the most haunted area of the building. The door to the third floor is always locked. One professor routinely checks that the door is locked. According to him, the door will be locked when he leaves for the night, but unlocked when he returns the next morning. Footsteps have also been heard coming from the third floor.

During a blizzard in February 2010, Jimmy Haines, with Hood College Facilities Division, was clearing snow when he saw a light in the third-floor window. With the bad weather, it was highly unlikely that anyone would be in the building let alone on the forbidden third floor. Others report seeing a red dot when looking into the windows at night, but have no explanation as to what it might be. A woman carrying a candle is also seen walking by the windows.

According to campus safety officer Douglas Young, not all the ghosts are seen at night. "Two of our guards watched [a] little girl walk from here down to the chapel, and then she just disappeared. That was in daylight."

UNIVERSITY OF MARYLAND
COLLEGE PARK, 20742

University of Maryland (UMD) at College Park has to be one of the most haunted colleges. And while almost every college claims a ghost story or two, UMD actually embraces its stories and even lists the haunted spots on its website and has an interactive map of the haunted locations.

Rossborough Inn was built in the early 1800s as a tavern and inn. It is the oldest building on campus and boasts several ghosts. The most famous is "Miss Bettie." She managed the inn during the Civil War.

In 1981 Larry Donnelly was working for dining services when he spotted Miss Bettie. He described her as wearing a long yellow gown similar to what was worn in the late 1800s. No one believed him until another employee spotted the woman exactly as Donnelly had described her. Since then other people have spotted her as well. Miss Bettie is also believed to open doors and turn off lights in the building. Her footsteps are heard on the second floor. Her face has also been seen reflected in mirrors and windows.

The Tawes Fine Arts Building was built in 1965. It is home to a ghost named "Mortimer." Legend says Mortimer was a dog killed in an accident in the theater during its construction. Since his death, the ghost has taken human form and haunts the building. Mortimer is blamed for footsteps heard walking through the empty theater as well as "practical jokes" played on people.

Hearing a piano playing isn't too odd, unless you're in Marie Mount Hall and you know there is no piano in the building. In the 1970s, night watchmen reported doors opening and closing and toilets flushing on their own. Matches would also be blown out inside the house, even though the doors and windows were closed. Most believe it is the ghost of the dean of College Home Economics, Marie Mount, who passed away in 1957.

Morrill Hall is home to a number of mysterious noises and smells. The sound of marching comes from outside the building, believed to be that of cadets, because the building is named after Justin S. Morrill. The Morrill Land Grant Act required military training, and students were often drilled in the field in front of Morrill Hall. The smell of smoke is also experienced here.

Len Bias still bounces his basketball in his old room in Washington Hall, according to some who have been awoken in the middle of the night by the sound. Bias died tragically of a cocaine overdose in his dorm room. He was celebrating his selection by the Boston Celtics in the 1986 NBA draft. Another student haunts Easton Hall. The student committed suicide in the building in 1991.

In the newspaper office in South Campus Dining Hall, a ghost cleans up after the editors. Books have been rearranged on the shelves and clutter has been cleaned up in the managing editor's office. In Stamp Student Union, the elevators have been known to move on their own. The building also has unexplained cold spots that many attribute to ghosts.

A campus employee was in H. J. Patterson Hall to do some routine maintenance work when he felt like someone was with him. He turned and saw a "strange, misshapen shadow dart across the wall." He was never able to attribute the shadow to anything living in the room. A woman wearing a dark dress and high heels has been seen in the Hornbake Library. When not seen, people report hearing the distinct sound of her heels walking across the linoleum floor.

Even the fraternity and sorority houses are haunted at the university. Delta Tau Delta is haunted by a fraternity brother who died in a car accident in 1955. He moves furniture and keeps a cabinet that once belonged to him warmer than the room. His face was once seen in a blank television screen. Alpha Omicron Pi sisters say computers operate and music plays without any human assistance. Their ghost also likes to knock things over. Finally, the founder of Kappa

Delta, Alma Preinkert, haunts its sorority house. She was murdered in her home by an intruder in 1954. Her unsolved murder may be the reason she haunts the grounds.

ST. JOHN'S AT PROSPECT HALL
889 BUTTERFLY LANE, FREDERICK, 21701

Walk up the staircase at St. John's at Prospect Hall and you may hear Agnes, the ghost of a seventeen-year-old indentured servant who died on the property. Agnes fell in love with her boss's son, Christopher Dulany. Upset at the idea of his son marrying below his station, Daniel Dulany sent Christopher to boarding school in Europe. Then, as if Agnes hadn't been punished enough, he walled her up (still alive) in the walls of the house.

"She turned off all the computers in my room one day," said Sandra Splaine in an interview for *Real Scary Stories*. "There's no way just the computers can be turned off without the lights and the Coke machine out in the hallway. And I was in a room with fifteen computers and they went off but nothing else went off." Agnes has also been known to turn lights on and off, open and close doors, and ring the school bells even when they are unplugged.

Many believe Agnes's bones are still within the walls of the school, but school officials are not eager to go looking for them. They feel the search would cost money better spent on more educational options. But they would also hate to prove the legend false, as they are fond of Agnes and her harmless pranks.

Agnes may not be alone. The ghost of General Joseph Hooker may have decided to join her. On June 28, 1863, Union General George Meade met with Hooker at the house. Meade was taking command of the Potomac Army. The action angered Hooker. As a result, on the anniversary of the event, his ghost is said to be seen floating around the dining room. His spirit has also been seen with his elbows on the desk and hands over his face as if despaired over the loss of his army (and his chance of fame at Gettysburg).

There is one problem with the story of Agnes and her lost love. The house was owned by Daniel Dulany the Younger from 1765 to 1772. In 1778, ownership was transferred to his son, Benjamin Tasker Dulany. Benjamin did have a brother, but his name was Daniel (the III). No record of any Charles Dulany exists. Also, Daniel Dulany, the elder, was well-known for coming to Maryland from Ireland as an indentured servant. It's possible that he managed to raise a son who would turn into a cruel jerk, but it seems unlikely. Of course, just because Agnes's backstory is wrong, doesn't mean her ghost isn't real.

Chapter 16
Prince George's County

Welcome to Prince George's County, which has some very unique haunted locations. First, there is a former dueling ground where citizens of the District of Columbia often faced off, including a couple who never left. Then there is the ghost of an eccentric old woman who didn't like anyone to use her parlor, even herself. Don't forget to stop by Six Flags America, one of the few theme parks with a real graveyard.

BLADENSBURG DUELING GROUNDS
CORNER OF BLADENSBURG ROAD AND THIRTY-EIGHTH AVENUE, COLMAR MANOR, 20722

Shadowy figures are seen wondering the Bladensburg Dueling Grounds. Most figures are indistinct but believed to be ghosts of the men who died on the "field of honor." Some figures are recognizable, and their stories make it easy to understand why their spirits might linger here.

Nowadays if someone offends you, you'd probably post about it on Facebook or send them a nasty tweet. But in the 1800s, offenses were taken more seriously. A man who felt slandered or insulted would challenge the offender to a duel. Not necessarily because he wanted to, but because society expected him to. A man was not a man without honor, and honor needed defending.

Dueling was a bloody, nasty, and sometimes ridiculous business. As a result, many areas, such as the District of Columbia, outlawed it, which required duelers to venture across state lines to designated dueling grounds. One such ground was located in Bladensburg, which is now haunted by some of the men who dueled there.

One of the earliest duels at Bladensburg occurred between two cousins: Armistead Thomson Mason and John Mason McCarty. The two quarreled over a Senate bill Mason had introduced. Although Mason's bill was defeated and he hoped to avoid a duel, McCarty continued to provoke him. Mason had no choice, and on February 6, 1819, the two men met. A bullet pierced Mason through the heart, killing him. He was thirty-two years old.

McCarty was wounded but survived the duel. The event troubled him greatly, however. He couldn't forgive himself for killing a relative he admired. He slowly went insane. For that reason, McCarty's ghost haunts the dueling grounds and not Mason's. His ghost is seen wandering near the spot where his cousin died, a confused look on his face.

Another ghost seen at the site is that of Congressman Jonathan Cilley. Cilley died after fighting a duel with Congressman William Graves. Graves had approached Cilley with a letter from newspaper editor James Webb. Cilley refused to take the letter, which Graves took as an insult and challenged Cilley to a duel. Before this incident, the two men never had any problems with each other.

Cilley was shot in the third round of the duel and died immediately, leaving a wife and three children behind. Cilley's ghost is reported to look very sad as a result of the events.

The last identifiable ghost is that of Commodore Stephen Decatur, a US naval officer known for numerous naval victories in the early nineteenth century. Decatur was challenged by Commodore James Barron.

Barron had commanded the USS *Chesapeake* on June 22, 1807, when it was stopped by the British frigate HMS *Leopard*. The British wanted to search for British Navy deserters, but Barron refused. The *Leopard* opened fire and killed three and wounded eight of *Chesapeake*'s crewmen.

Feeling unprepared for battle, Barron surrendered. The British refused the surrender. Instead, they boarded the ship and took away four men they claimed were deserters, only one of whom was actually British. Americans along with President Jefferson were outraged, and the event contributed to the War of 1812.

The event had severe consequence for Barron. He was court-martialed and found guilty for "neglecting on the probability of an engagement, to clear his ship for action." He was sentenced to a five-year suspension from the Navy without pay. Decatur, who had been one of the judges for the court-martial, was given the command of the *Chesapeake*.

When the War of 1812 began, Barron tried to get his old job back, but was refused. At the time, Barron was in Copenhagen, and he didn't have the funds to return to America until 1819. Upon his return he learned of some negative comments Decatur had made about him. The two exchanged correspondences that eventually led to the two men facing each other in a duel.

Early on the morning of March 22, 1820, the two men arrived at Bladensburg. Both men hit their targets, but although Decatur's wounds were fatal, Barron survived his. Over ten thousand people paid their respects to Decatur before his burial. His ghost has been seen at Bladensburg, but can be found more often at his former house on Lafayette Square in Washington DC.

MOUNT AIRY MANSION
8714 ROSARYVILLE ROAD, UPPER MARLBORO, 20772

Miss Eleanor Calvert was known for being eccentric and stubborn. She insisted on doing things her own way and living on her own terms. At age eighty-one she insisted on staying in her family's ancestral home, Mount Airy Mansion. She always kept the front parlor locked, because she didn't like it to be used. She also insisted on using old-fashioned oil lamps at night, although everyone warned her it was dangerous.

She learned how dangerous it could be on July 5, 1902, when she fell while carrying a lamp. The lamp set her clothes on fire. Eleanor managed to extinguish the flames but not before suffering severe burns. She lay in her home for twelve hours before being discovered and getting help. She passed away a few days later.

As was the custom of the time, her casket was brought back to her home for the wake. Family members decided to place it in the front parlor. After all, Eleanor couldn't object to it being used now that she was gone.

Shortly before the funeral was to begin, a staff member discovered the door was locked. The door required a key to be locked or unlocked, but when they went to the hallway table where the key was kept, they discovered it missing.

They surveyed everyone, but no one had the key or knew who had locked the door.

As the search for the key continued, family members and guests reported hearing "strange noises" coming from the parlor. They grew increasingly alarmed as the noises continued behind the locked door. Finally they decided to break into the room. As soon as the door opened, the noises stopped. No one, except Eleanor, was in the room and nothing had been disturbed. Only one thing was different about the room. Sitting on the table beside Eleanor's coffin was the missing key.

Eleanor continues to haunt Mount Airy. After her death, trustees for the estate decided to sell the property and all of its contents. Tillie Duvall purchased the property in 1903. Soon after she moved in, she experienced a number of paranormal experiences recorded by John Martin Hammond in his 1914 book *Colonial Mansions of Maryland and Delaware.*

Duvall was woken up in the middle of the night by a ghostly woman who "put its cold hands around her throat." She also reported no lamps would stay lit in a room above the dining room. No matter what lamp they used, as soon as it crossed the threshold, it would go out. She also experienced doors opening and closing on their own and watched the bed sag and creak when no one was near them.

Another ghost wanders the gardens of the house. She is believed to be Ariana Calvert, daughter of Benedict Calvert. Legend says Ariana had fallen in love with a young man that her father did not approve of. Her family forced her to end the relationship and send him away. Ariana immediately regretted her actions. She died of a broken heart at age twenty-five. Her ghost is waiting in vain for her love to return to her.

Ariana's father was responsible for expanding the house into what stands today. He had inherited the property from his father. After it was sold in 1903, the house was owned by Tillie Duvall and became a country inn known as Dower House. The entire house was gutted by a fire in 1931. It sat until purchased by Cissy Patterson, who restored the house. She bequeathed the house to Ann Bowie Smith, who sold it to the State of Maryland. It is now part of Rosaryville State Park.

The house itself remained empty until the 1980s, when it was renovated to be used for private events. Construction workers claimed to have a number of experiences in the house during this time. Two workers were in the house after dusk when they observed a door open on its own. They immediately closed the door, only to watch it open a second time. The two workers examined the hinges and latch, but found no reason for the door not to remain closed. Another worker reported seeing a figure standing in a second-story window when he arrived early one morning. However, it would have been impossible for anyone to have been standing there, as there was no floor in that room.

MONTPELIER MANSION
9650 MUIRKIRK ROAD, LAUREL, 20708

In 1968 a caretaker at Montpelier Mansion was working when he saw the figure of a woman. The building was closed to visitors, so he went to confront her. When he got closer, he immediately recognized her from her portrait on the wall, which increased his tension. Ann Ridgley Snowden had died in 1834.

The caretaker wasn't the first—or last—person to see a ghost at the mansion. Cleaven Woods, an employee of the mansion for thirty years, saw a woman in eighteenth-century clothing in the passageway and in a downstairs bedroom. However, the other female ghost in the house, who is unidentified, appears on the main stairway. She is wrapped in a quilt. Once she walks up the stairs, she disappears through the wall. She's been known to look directly at people and walk through them should they be standing in her way.

Another ghost in the house is a young girl who peers out one of the second-story windows. Ann's son has also been seen riding toward the front of the house on horseback, usually in autumn. The mansion also boasts a few famous ghosts: George and Martha Washington and Thomas Jefferson. While all three had stayed at the house in their lifetimes, no real connection or explanation as to why they would return to haunt it has been found.

But it is the unseen ghost that causes the most trouble. He (or she) locks doors and cabinets, causing all sorts of problems for people. Montpelier Mansion was built in the late 1700s by Thomas Snowden. It currently serves as a museum and rental facility.

OAKLANDS

13700 OAKLANDS MANOR DRIVE, LAUREL, 20708

A couple miles down the road is another house associated with Thomas Snowden that some claim is more haunted.

Snowden built the house as a wedding gift for his daughter. Whether or not it is more haunted than Oaklands is debatable, but it does seem to have more stories associated with it.

Oaklands was once a magnificent mansion on over a thousand acres. In the 1900s it started to fall into disrepair, and land around it was sold to a development. It currently sits in the center of a modern housing development. Still, the modern setting hasn't decreased the ghost stories associated with the house.

Major Richard Contee is one of the few ghosts whose identity is known. Contee lived in the house after he served in the Civil War. The war changed him, and he displayed increasingly erratic behavior, which is why he is known as the "mad major." People have reported seeing his ghost wandering around the grounds, and a paranormal investigation recorded an EVP that sounds like someone saying "Major Contee."

A young boy dressed in a brown suit and a rounded collar is also seen at Oaklands. His identity is unknown, but some speculate he may be Major Contee's son. Other figures seen at Oaklands include a large black woman and a black man believed to be two of the over two hundred slaves who once lived at Oaklands and a woman in a hoop skirt.

Then there are the unseen ghosts. Between eight and nine each night, hooves galloping up the driveway can be heard, followed by the sound of footsteps entering the house. Then, after a few moments, footsteps are heard leaving, followed by the sound of the horse departing as well.

A farmhand, Jon Harzer, experienced something similar when he found himself in the house by himself one night in

1977. He was sitting in the living room watching TV while waiting for the owner, John Pecor, to return when he heard footsteps coming down the stairs. He assumed Pecor had returned earlier and gone upstairs without him knowing it. The footsteps continued into the dining room, which was between the living room and the staircase.

"I heard footfalls come into the dining room and leaned forward on the couch," Harzer recalled in an interview. "Looking into the dining room, I was ready to give John grief about how long he had been gone [but] I saw no one. The footsteps continued on and then stopped!"

Probably the most disturbing paranormal event at Oaklands is the feeling of being watched or followed while on the property. People often find themselves looking for the cause of the feeling, only to discover they are alone (or at least that is how it appears).

SIX FLAGS AMERICA
13710 Central Avenue, Upper Marlboro, 20774

What does a theme park do when it discovers it's haunted? Turns it into an attraction (sponsored by Milky Way or Snickers—I kid you not). Although the attraction is an October event, and most of the scares are manufactured, the legend behind it is as real as the central figure of the story: Eleanor Hall.

Eleanor Hall died on July 17, 1702, at the age of five. Her parents, Benjamin and Mary, buried her behind Hall Manor. Some stories state she was older, that she died on June 15, or that she died on her birthday. According to *Stones and*

Bones: Cemetery Records of Prince George's County, Maryland, her tombstone records that she died at the age of five years and nine months and lists her date of death as July 17. (The birthday myth is promoted by Six Flags October event.)

It seems anything bad that happens in the park is attributed to Eleanor, even events that are not paranormal. The many things Eleanor is believed to have done include momentarily turning off the power in the park, flipping a raft, starting a car fire, and so on.

She is even believed to have caused a boy to drown in a wave pool on the anniversary of her death. However, there is no record of a boy dying in the wave pool on June 15, July 17, or any other day. In fact, no deaths have been reported for this park.

Staff have reported hearing giggling and other vocalizations after the park has closed and the children have gone home, but nothing substantial. Your best chance to see Eleanor is to go during October for Six Flags' "Haunting of Hall Manor" haunted backwoods trail, which does promise (for an additional fee) that visitors are "likely to come face-to-face with Eleanor herself."

FOREST HAVEN INSANE ASYLUM
3398 CENTER AVENUE, LAUREL, 20724

Abandoned medical institutions are ripe for ghost stories. They look creepy and can produce backstories horrific (and sometimes even true) enough to produce nightmares in the bravest souls. But separating truth from fiction is difficult. Imaginations run away with visitors to the sites and everything they see or experience is marked down as "paranormal." Similar to the dogs in the movie *Up*, but instead of yelling "Squirrel!" they yell "Ghost!"

That seems to be the case for both Forest Haven Asylum and Glenn Dale Hospital.

Forest Haven is haunted, but not necessarily by ghosts. Sometimes referred to as Forest Haven Insane Asylum or just Forest Haven Asylum, it was opened in 1925 as a progressive institute that aspired to teach usable skills to people with mental illnesses and intellectual disabilities. By the 1960s, Forest Haven had transformed from a progressive place to a house of horrors. Patients were exposed to unspeakable abuse. A class-action suit was filed in 1975 by relatives of some of the patients, but that wasn't enough to change things. Finally in 1991, Forest Haven closed its doors.

Rather than pack up and move items to other locations, the site was abandoned. Furniture, appliances, medical equipment, even arcade games and vending machines were all left behind. Over the decades the buildings have decayed and everything is now covered with a brown layer of dust.

And while many claim that the facility is haunted by the numerous patients who died horrible deaths here, no credible stories seem to be circulating. Still, as you look at Forest Haven today and read about its history, you have to wonder how it could not be haunted.

Still, caution should be taken by anyone who ventures to Forest Haven today. The buildings still "stand" but are crumbling. The site is located on federal park land and patrolled by security guards day and night. As to what you'll see, nothing specific seems to be mentioned when people discuss the location. Just that it's "haunted."

Stories about Glenn Dale are a little easier to find. A neighbor to the property heard gunshots and called the police. They found one of their officers frozen in terror unable to speak. All the rounds in his gun had been fired into the wall he was staring at, but nothing was there. Another legend speaks of a ghost who haunts the hospital wearing a straightjacket. He went insane after his wife and children were murdered before his eyes during a home invasion. Apparently the straightjacket didn't help, as he managed to break into the pharmacy and kill himself with pills. The suicide has bound his spirit to the hospital.

Others report seeing ghostly patients wandering the floors, smoke coming from the long-defunct crematorium, and even a ghostly pack of dogs roaming the grounds. People report hearing banging, yelling, screams, and even laughter coming from the buildings.

GLENN DALE HOSPITAL
5201 GLENN DALE ROAD, GLENN DALE, 20769

Glenn Dale was built in 1934 in what was at the time a rural location. It has always been a hospital and has no horrific tales associated with it like Forest Haven does. It was closed in 1982 due to asbestos. It has sat empty, although it was purchased in 1994 by Maryland-National Capital Park and Planning Commission, which is more interested in finding a buyer for the site than exploring its paranormal possibilities.

For some reason no one wants to spend several million dollars on property with buildings that are unstable but can't be demolished (it's a registered historic site). Not to mention the amount of asbestos and debris that needs to be removed. Oh, and they require that a majority of the property be used for continuing care or a retirement home.

The place is rumored to be haunted. One group on a ghost hunt claim they saw a woman looking out of one of the windows. Whenever they tried to take her picture, she disappeared behind the frame and all they got was a "white glowing image."

Although it may be tempting, ghost hunting here is unadvisable unless you would like to become a ghost yourself. Becoming the first ghost-hunting ghost sounds appealing, but there are other sites more haunted and easier to access that you can visit without being arrested for trespassing.

Chapter 17

Montgomery County Houses

Montgomery County is the most populated county in Maryland. Before moving here, a person would be wise to check that the former occupants moved out. This county has a higher-than-normal haunted house count.

ANNINGTON MANOR
24001 White's Ferry Road, Dickerson, 20842

The Battle of Ball's Bluff is not the most famous battle of the Civil War, but it is infamous for the numerous errors that caused a monumental Union defeat. It started when Captain Chase Philbrick mistook a line of trees for a Confederate encampment. Then, the troops sent over to "attack" the trees stumbled across a company of Confederate infantry, resulting in a real battle. Colonel Edward Baker decided to use his troops as reinforcement, but he only had four small boats to transport them over the Potomac River. When Baker was killed that afternoon, the Union troops crumbled. The Confederates drove the Union troops over the bluff and into the river.

The Union suffered approximately 1,000 casualties; the Confederates only had 155 casualties. The loss was monumental for Abraham Lincoln since Baker was a close personal friend. The night before the battle, Baker had had dinner with Robert Smoot, who owned Annington Manor.

Although the battle took place on the Virginia side of the Potomac, Baker's ghost along with other Civil War soldiers have been seen around the house and along the C & O Canal. During renovations at Annington, workmen reported seeing a man wearing an old-fashioned uniform riding a black horse. Others simply report hearing hoofbeats galloping around the property.

BEALL-DAWSON HOUSE
103 WEST MONTGOMERY AVENUE, ROCKVILLE, 20850

In the 1980s Rae Koch was dipping candles in the Beall-Dawson house when she noticed a black man kneeling by the door of the carriage house laying bricks. Before she could say anything, the man vanished. That area of the floor had been laid in the 1940s by Nathan Briggs. Sadly, he committed suicide shortly after completing the work. Many speculate that it may be his ghost haunting that spot.

The ghost also could have been one of the many slaves who built the house for Upton Beall in 1815. The house remained in the Beall family until 1960, when Amelia Somervell Dawson moved into the house. The house is now the headquarters of the Montgomery County Historical Society, which admits that strange things happen in the house. For example, the security alarm frequently gets triggered in the middle of the night. However, when police investigate, nothing is ever found.

Employees hear strange, unexplained noises in the house. Most have heard footsteps walking around the house, even though no one else is in the building. The sounds are usually near the stairs or a second-story room that once housed the library. One volunteer, after hearing footsteps in the house, went to investigate. She found no one in the house, but somehow a platter that had been placed on a side dish was now sitting in the center of the table.

Then there is the dollhouse. It had been given to a former resident of the house as a birthday present. Sadly, the girl died a few years later. Staff in the house noticed that the furniture in the house was constantly being moved, even when no one had access to the house. When someone decided to remove the delicate furniture from the dollhouse, people began hearing wailing coming from the dollhouse, like that of a child crying. Apparently even ghostly children can throw tantrums.

GREENWOOD HOUSE
21315 Georgia Avenue, Brookeville, 20833

The Greenwood House has one of the most unique ghosts, or a "poultry-geist" as some call it. Apparently, one summer a chicken snuck into the house. The family was busy getting ready to go on vacation and didn't notice it. The chicken ended up locked in the house while the family was away and died in the attic. Since then, people report hearing a chicken pecking and scratching there. Another animal ghost is that of a Newfoundland. The dog lived at the estate prior to the Civil War. He was found dead in a field one day, apparently killed by someone who was never caught. He was so beloved that he was buried in the family cemetery. His ghost is seen roaming the fields surrounding the property.

Several human ghosts also haunt the property. An older woman with white hair dressed in a nineteenth-century-style, blue-and-white dress is believed to be the ghost of Rebecca Davis. She is seen standing in the doorway of the Blue Room. The bed in the Blue Room always appears rumpled, as if someone had been sleeping in it, even after it is made. Guests who stay in the room report being woken in the middle of the night by someone shaking their shoulder. They also report hearing their name called and the sound of chains rattling.

The house was built in 1721, and a number of slaves lived and worked on the property. When the Civil War was over and the slaves were freed, a dairymaid named Charlotte became so excited that she suffered a stroke and died the following day, never experiencing the freedom she had just acquired. She was buried in the old Slave Cemetery behind the barn. Her ghost now wanders the property, continually seeking the freedom that was denied her.

THOMAS-BENTLEY (MADISON) HOUSE
205 MARKET STREET, BROOKEVILLE, 20833

On August 26, 1814, during the War of 1812, President James Madison arrived at the house of Caleb and Henrietta Bentley. He had been forced to flee DC after the British invasion. Madison spent one night in the house before heading out. That one night was enough for the estate to be forever known as the Madison House, now also known as the Thomas-Bentley House.

Most of the ghost stories associated with the house come from the Archer family, who owned the house in the 1950s. A maid working in the house reported hearing a door in the attic open and close, followed by loud footsteps running down the stairs and another door opening and closing. A few minutes later the pattern repeated, only in reverse. At first she assumed one of the children was playing, until she realized that they were at school. She went upstairs to investigate, but no one else was in the house.

On another occasion, a friend of the family watched as her door opened and closed and then the bed sank down. It appeared as if someone had entered the room and sat on the bed. Then, as if the ghost realized the room was occupied, the indention disappeared and the door opened and closed. Another guest continually had problems with the bedcovers being pulled off her in the middle of the night.

One snowy day the Archer children decided to use a Ouija Board to communicate with the ghost. The board gave them a name: Nancy Helen Riggs. Later that spring, they stumbled across a neglected family cemetery while exploring. Inside they found a gravestone that read "Nancy Helen Riggs."

FAIR HILL

As a Quaker, Colonel Richard Brooke was supposed to be a pacifist. So when he decided to fight in the Revolutionary War, he was expelled from the community. When he died, he was refused burial in the Sandy Spring Friends Meeting-house graveyard and buried at his estate, Fair Hill.

Brooke's spirit was not at peace, though. People reported hearing a man on horseback riding around the property. The sound would be heard during the day as well as at night. Everyone knew it was him, because on stormy nights he would be seen riding a headless horse through the neighborhood and up the staircase of his former house.

Three other ghosts also resided at Fair Hill Farm. Margaret Kirk's ghost was often seen sitting on the top of the stairs of the house. She was five years old when she died of diphtheria in 1862. A baby who died in the fireplace (either accidentally or on purpose) also haunted the house. Crying was heard coming from the wall behind the fireplace. Then, there was the Irishman who haunted the cellar of the building.

Fair Hill Farm was burned to the ground on May 1, 1977. The fire occurred days after the current owner had been evicted. His loan had been acquired by Dominic F. Antonelli, who planned to put up a shopping center. The house was in the way. Not so coincidentally, a historic barn burned to ground less than a week later. Both fires were ruled arson, but no one was ever caught.

With the historic property out of the way, nothing prevented the shopping center from being built. It is now the Olney Village Center. Interestingly, a year later Antonelli was indicted on charges of bribery. It seemed he had given money to a DC official. Although originally found guilty, he was granted a retrial and acquitted the second time around.

OLNEY HOUSE
3308 OLNEY SANDY SPRING ROAD, OLNEY, 20832

A little girl about twelve years old named Nancy haunts Olney House, now known as Ricciuti's. Nancy died during a hunting accident and may have been the illegitimate daughter of one of the owners of the house. Olney House dates back to the early 1800s. Nancy has been known to turn on all the faucets and move things around when no one is there.

One customer was leaving with her own daughter when the child pointed to one of the dormer windows claiming to see a little girl. But her mother was unable to see anything when she looked.

According to owner James Ricciuti, a canine unit was sent into the restaurant after the alarm went off. When the police arrived, the door was standing open. They tracked someone through the house and into the attic. But no one was discovered in the attic, nor would there have been any way for someone to get out of the attic without passing the police. Workers frequently hear the sound of someone rocking in the attic, even though there is no rocker located there.

The haunting didn't begin when Ricciuti's opened. Before it was a restaurant, it had been divided into six small shops. Shop owners reported numerous unexplained happenings, like hand mirrors that flipped over and curling irons that heated up on their own in the beauty shop. A bookstore had problems with a statue of the Virgin Mary that was always being turned so that it faced the wall.

MARWOOD MANSION
11231 River View Drive, Potomac, 20854

Marwood Mansion is the new kid on the block, as it was built in 1931. Toilets inside the house often flush for no reason. Steam has been seen coming from the bathtub, even though the water isn't running, and a bathroom window raises itself. These things may be caused by a butler whose ghostly form has been seen walking around the property.

Marwood was once owned by relatives of the Gore family. It was also rented in the 1930s by Joseph Kennedy, John F. Kennedy's father. Franklin Roosevelt also rented the house as a summer retreat. In 2011 the property was purchased by Ted Leonsis, owner of the Washington Capitals and Washington Wizards.

If you ever stay at Marwood, be sure not to leave anything in the basement overnight. Boxes left in the basement overnight are found the following morning ransacked with many of the items destroyed. Another odd thing that happens here involves white cracks that appear in the marble, only to disappear later.

BLAIR MANSION
7711 Eastern Avenue, Silver Spring, 20912

Blair Mansion was a wedding present from Abner Shoemaker to his niece Abigail in the late 1800s. Sadly, her husband gambled and the property had to be sold at tax auction ten years later. And while circumstances may have forced

Abigail out of the house during her life, she's returned and made it clear she has no intention of leaving.

Through the years the house has changed ownership. Eventually it was transformed into a restaurant. But through it all, Abigail has made her presence known. Abigail likes to turn lights on and off in the house, move things around, and knock things off the walls. She's even managed to set off the door chime numerous times, even though it is motion sensitive.

According to Raymon Zeender, one Sunday night he and a musician who had been playing at the mansion were closing up. Zeender asked the musician to turn off the lights on the second floor. The musician happily complied. When he came back downstairs, he told Zeender all the lights were off except in the room being cleaned. Zeender told him no cleaners were scheduled. The musician insisted he saw a lady with a bucket and broom, but upon inspection no one was on the second floor.

COUNSELMAN FARMHOUSE
Bradley Boulevard, Rockville, 20850

Two former residents haunt the Counselman Farmhouse in Rockville according to Dennis William Hauck's book *Haunted Places: The National Directory*. One is Rosie B. Counselman, who committed suicide in the house on April 29, 1969. The other is Jack Peyton, who died there in 1976. Although he doesn't give specifics on what they do, a house sitter fled in terror after a ghostly encounter. The house has been part of an October ghost tour operated by the Montgomery County Historical Society.

Part 5

SOUTHERN

Southern Maryland refers to the area on the western shore of the Chesapeake Bay. It includes Calvert, Charles, and St. Mary's Counties. Located south of Washington DC, the area remains mostly rural, except in the northern areas where the DC suburbs have slowly encroached.

John Wilkes Booth traveled through this area after assassinating Abraham Lincoln. Lincoln's assassination created quite a few ghosts, including a couple of them in this area. Point Lookout is another historic haunted site both for its lighthouse and the former Civil War prison camp once located there. This area also has not one, but two, haunted rocks.

Chapter 18

Lincoln Assassination Conspirators

On April 14, 1865, John Wilkes Booth shot President Abraham Lincoln and set off a series of events that destroyed several families, including that of Mary Surratt. As he made his escape, Booth stopped at two different houses in Maryland: Mary Surratt's and Dr. Mudd's. This helped get both of them tried as conspirators in the assassination. Today, both locations are haunted with ghosts still trying to prove their innocence.

During the Civil War, Mary Surratt was facing her own set of difficulties that had little to do with the war. Her husband, John, died in 1862, leaving the family in debt. The home she lived in was also a tavern and inn, but with the war on, her patrons had difficulty paying her.

In October 1864 she leased her home to a former policeman, John Lloyd, and move to a townhouse that the family owned in Washington DC. She turned it into a boardinghouse, which provided her enough income with which to live. She wouldn't live there for long.

On April 17, 1865, she was arrested at her Washington boardinghouse. Metro police had arrived at her house late that night. While they were there, Lewis Powell (Paine/ Payne) arrived, claiming he was there to dig a gutter. While Booth was killing Lincoln, Powell had attempted to do the same to Secretary of State William Seward. He had been accompanied by David Herold, who fled while Powell was in the house. Having no knowledge of Washington, Powell wandered around for three days before returning to Surratt's boardinghouse to enlist aid. Surratt denied knowing him. The metro police noticed that Powell's nice clothes, manicured nails, and lack of calluses did not fit with his story that he was a common laborer. Then there was the fact that his clothes were blood stained.

Powell's arrival sealed Surratt's fate, and they were both arrested and eventually tried for conspiring with Booth to assassinate Lincoln. Quite a few people were also arrested for conspiring to assassinate Lincoln, but most of them were released. Besides Mary, Herold, and Powell, only five would eventually stand trial:

George Atzerodt: He was assigned with the task of killing Vice President Andrew Johnson, but went drinking instead. Ironically, he was arrested after he was overheard boasting about contributing to the assassination.

Dr. Samuel Mudd: He set Booth's broken leg after the assassination.

Edman Spangler: He was accused of helping Booth escape from Ford's Theatre.

Michael O'Laughlen: A childhood friend of Booth's, he turned himself into authorities.

Samuel Arnold: Another friend of Booth's, he was not even in Washington during the assassination, and his role in the conspiracy is unclear.

The trial began on May 12, 1865, and ended on July 5, 1865. The next day the public learned of the conspirator's fate. Herold, Powell, Atzerodt, and Surratt were all sentenced to death. Spangler received six years, while the other three received life sentences.

Surratt's sentence was carried out on July 7, 1865. She was the only one who received the death sentence who was not directly involved in an assassination attempt. Of the four that went to prison, O'Laughlen died while in prison. President Johnson pardoned the other three in 1869.

Lincoln's assassination changed history and set off a series of events that seems to have created quite a few ghosts. At least two of them are located in Maryland.

SURRATT HOUSE MUSEUM
9118 BRANDYWINE ROAD, CLINTON, 20735

Mary Surratt lived in the house in Clinton from 1852 until 1864, when she rented it to John Lloyd. The house wasn't just her home; it was also a tavern, hotel, and local post office. Originally the area was called Surrattsville, after the postmaster, John Surratt, Mary's husband. After Mary's trial, the town's name was changed to Robeysville and then later to Clinton.

Tales of ghosts at the Surratt house have been circulating since the 1940s. At the time, the widow who owned the house was renting out half of it. She and some of her tenants claimed to see Mary Surratt's ghost on the staircase landing between the first and second floors and heard disembodied voices coming from the back of the house. Mary's spirit has also been seen on the porch.

After the Maryland-National Capital Parks and Planning Commission acquired the house in 1965, new ghost stories emerged. One tour guide claimed to have seen a young girl in Victorian clothing smoothing out the bed linens and then peering under the bed as if looking for something. The teenage daughter of another tour guide saw a bearded man reflected in a mirror. He was sitting in one of the rocking chairs. When she turned to look directly at him, he had disappeared.

At least two sets of footsteps are heard in the house. On the first floor, heavy footsteps like those made using work boots are heard. A lighter set of footsteps are heard coming from the second-floor bedrooms and in the hallway. The smell of tobacco is also experienced, although the building is nonsmoking. On the back stairs of the tavern, the vague figures of men have been seen in hushed conversation, and excited voices have been heard in the building.

In an online message board, Laurie Verge, director of the Surratt House Museum, wrote that she had heard the sound of heavy work boots in the house. According to her, "Our theory is that it's John Lloyd, who has been doomed to spend eternity here for betraying his landlady." She also said that a television director claimed that he was "shoved by unseen forces in the family dining room at the house."

Verge also said that the house has been investigated by two mediums, and both declared that there were no ghosts.

DR. SAMUEL A. MUDD'S HOUSE
3725 Dr. Samuel Mudd Road, Waldorf, 20601

After John Wilkes Booth shot Lincoln in Ford's Theatre, he attempted a dashing escape by jumping onto the stage, shouting, *"Sic semper tyrannis,"* Latin for "Thus always to tyrants." He ended up catching his heel on some fabric draped around Lincoln's box and breaking his leg. He still managed to shout the words (although Booth later wrote he shouted the words before he shot Lincoln, witnesses all reported he said the words—or something similar—after he landed on the stage) before limping away.

He managed to hobble to his horse and escape from DC. After meeting up with David Herold, he stopped at Mary Surratt's former house to get a gun John Lloyd had hidden for him weeks earlier. Herold and Booth then traveled seventeen miles to the home of Dr. Samuel A. Mudd. They arrived at 4 a.m. on April 15.

Mudd set Booth's leg and then sent him to an upstairs bedroom to rest. Later that afternoon the two men left. Mudd had learned about the assassination, but did not bother to contact the authorities until the following day. When questioned, Mudd denied knowing Booth, although witnesses later testified that Booth and Mudd had met before.

George Atzerodt also told authorities that Booth had told him he had sent "liquor and provisions" to Dr. Mudd's house two weeks before the murder. All of this was enough to convict Dr. Mudd as a conspirator to the assassination. He escaped being sentenced to death by one vote and instead was sentenced to life in prison.

While in prison at Fort Jefferson, there was an outbreak of yellow fever that killed the prison doctor. Mudd took over the position and helped stop the spread of the disease. Afterward, soldiers at the fort petitioned President Johnson about Mudd's assistance. It would be over a year before President Johnson pardoned Mudd.

After his release Mudd returned to his farm and resumed his practice. He died in 1883 at the age of forty-nine. In

1951 Mudd's grandson started a campaign to prove his grandfather's innocence, but he was unsuccessful.

Dr. Mudd's former house has been turned into a museum, and some believe his spirit lingers in an effort to one day clear his name. One of the most common unexplained happenings involves the bed located in the room where Booth rested. According to Danny Fluhart, president of the Samuel A. Mudd Society, no one is allowed to touch the bed. But despite this, they continually enter the room and find the bed messed up, as if someone had lain down on the bed. This happens when no one is in the building, like after they have closed for the night. They'll return the following morning and find the bed rumpled.

People have also claimed to see shadowy figures moving inside the house, hearing disembodied voices, and finding books and photos moved with no explanation. Some visitors say they have felt someone tapping their back or hand. One paranormal investigator touring the house took a picture that shows a shadowy figure descending the staircase in a mirror, even though no one was on the stairs when she took it.

The Atlantic Paranormal Society (TAPS) investigated the house during season 5 of their show *Ghost Hunters*. While there, they claim to have picked up the EVP of a man's voice saying, "I am not guilty." Of course everyone believed it was Mudd reaching out to plead his case from the beyond.

Chapter 19

Point Lookout

Point Lookout is at the southern tip of St. Mary's County on a peninsula between the Potomac River and Chesapeake Bay. It got its name in the War of 1812, when it was used as a lookout for British ships. It wasn't until 1830 that a lighthouse was built here. The lighthouse has been called "America's Most Haunted Lighthouse." Some credit the Civil War hospital and prison built near the lighthouse for helping it achieve that status.

LIGHTHOUSE

11175 POINT LOOKOUT ROAD, SCOTLAND, 20687

The Point Lookout Lighthouse was first lit on September 20, 1830, by the first keeper, James Davis. Davis died a few months later, and his daughter, Ann Davis, took over the job. She remained keeper until 1847. The next keeper, William Wood, had a few problems with the job. His cat fell into a barrel of lamp oil, contaminating fifty-six gallons of valuable fuel. The cat also broke two dozen glass lamp chimneys. Wood lost over a year's wages as a result.

Other keepers took over and at least two of them died while on duty. A number of ships have also wrecked near the lighthouse, including one in 1878, which seems to have caused some of the haunted phenomena here.

In October 1878, a fierce storm made its way up the East Coast. When it reached Chesapeake Bay, winds had reached hurricane force, causing immense waves to break over the upper deck of the steamer *Express* off the coast of Point Lookout. The winds eventually flipped the ship on her side and then rolled it over. Survivors gathered timber to make an escape raft. One officer, Joseph Haney, plunged through the skylight when the boat overturned. His body was found several days later on the shore and buried nearby. He was described as being twenty-five years old, clean shaven, and wearing a brown overcoat and blue sack coat.

People began to report seeing his ghost roaming the beaches of Point Lookout. A resident in the lighthouse would often hear a knocking on the door. When he opened it, Haney's ghost would disappear toward the bay, leaving a puddle of water behind.

In 1977, Gerald Sword had a similar experience that he later told in an article for the St. Mary's County Historical Society. Sword was at his kitchen table with his dog during a strong storm when he got the feeling he was being watched. His dog suddenly got up and ran to the door. Sword turned and saw a "young clean-shaven white male peering through the window . . . He had on a floppy cap, an opened dark-colored sack coat, dark hair about collar length and dark eyes."

He went over to the door and pulled it open and watched the man turn and disappear through the screening on the porch. Two years later he was researching shipwrecks that had occurred in the area when he came across a newspaper account of the report that included a description of Haney, which matched the man he saw.

Sword also reported that doors opened and shut mysteriously in the lighthouse. He often heard footsteps, human voices talking lowly, coughing, snoring, and the sound of objects crashing—although he never found a source for any of the sounds. He also reported feeling invisible entities walking past him and the feeling that he was being watched.

Laura Berg was the last resident of the lighthouse and also had experiences there. According to Berg, the day after she moved in, she heard footsteps walking back and forth in the hallway outside her door. "It sounded like heavy shoes with thick heels or boots. They just kept walking up and down."

She also had problems with an odor in the middle room that she had turned into a guest room. It smelled as if something was dead inside the room. But the odor only occurred at night. No matter how much she scrubbed and sprayed air freshener, the odor would reoccur each night.

In 1980 Sword, who was park manager at the time, came to help her find out what was going on. They reached out to the Maryland Committee for Psychical Research. They arrived to do an investigation of the house and later returned to perform a séance. During their investigation a picture of Nancy Stallings, a medium with the Maryland Committee, was taken in one of the bedrooms. In the photo a figure appears to Nancy's right. No one in the bedroom at the time remembers seeing the figure. Many describe the figure as a "headless Confederate soldier leaning against the wall."

The photo can be found on ptlookoutlighthouse.com, a site dedicated to the history (including paranormal history) of the lighthouse. The photo is incredibly grainy and nothing in the image is in focus. While there definitely looks like a man standing next to the medium, the man looks strangely two-dimensional. And while he may be headless, it is because that portion is cut off in the photo and not because his head isn't there.

One must ask why a Confederate soldier's ghost would be in the lighthouse. While there was a prison nearby during the Civil War, the lighthouse was still a lighthouse. Pamela Edwards was the keeper from 1855 to 1869. Why would a prisoner have been brought to the lighthouse during this time?

Legend says that Union officials housed female prisoners inside the lighthouse before they could be transferred to a federal prison. One room of the lighthouse may even have been used as an interrogation room. This may explain why a man in a soldier's uniform would appear inside the house.

Other "ghostly" photos are also posted on ptlookout lighthouse.com. Most of them are of orbs. One interesting one was taken on April 4, 2009, by Natalia Parra. In the photo a man wearing a hat and vest or poncho can be seen through the window of the door. It is clearly not a person, because while the body is very distinct, the head and face are hard to make out and almost translucent.

CIVIL WAR PRISON

During the Civil War, in 1862, most of the land around the lighthouse was occupied with a Union Army hospital, an army garrison at Fort Lincoln, and a prisoner-of-war camp. The prison camp came into being after the Battle of Gettysburg. It would eventually hold twenty thousand men, although it was designed to hold half that number. In the three years the prison existed, more than fifty thousand Confederate prisoners would pass through the gates of the prison.

The Union didn't bother to build permanent housing for the prisoners, but simply provided them with tents. The tents proved inadequate protection against the heat of summer and cold of winter. Contaminated water, meager rations, along with a number of diseases such as smallpox, tuberculosis, malaria, and typhoid fever were all problems at the overcrowded camp. Official records say that around four thousand Confederate prisoners died during the war, but some estimate that the number could be closer to eight thousand or even fourteen thousand.

Eventually, the remains of Union soldiers who died in the hospital were removed to Arlington National Cemetery outside of Washington DC. The two Confederate cemeteries that existed remained until 1870, when 3,384 of the remains were transferred to a new site, now known as Point Lookout Confederate Cemetery. Since identification of individual remains was impossible, they were buried in a mass grave. The site is marked by a twenty-five-foot white marble obelisk.

Whether it was the terrible circumstances they experienced during their life or the horrible treatment they received after death, it seems a number of Confederates have returned to Point Lookout.

Park ranger Don Hammett saw "the form of a man running toward the woods away . . . at full speed using long strides." At first he thought it was a trespasser or someone up to no good. But he couldn't find any signs of a person having crossed the road. He sighted this figure several times, always at the same spot. He believes it to be the ghost of a man who was trying to escape from the smallpox hospital nearby.

Others report seeing a figure of a man in uniform running across the road in their rearview mirror. He may have been one of the Confederate prisoners who attempted to escape by faking illness. They found it easier to escape from the hospital than the prison.

Others claim that a young man dressed in a Confederate uniform has appeared in the backseat of their car. He remains until you pass the Confederate Cemetery. Two teenagers were driving through the park when they saw a man dressed like a soldier patrolling inside the fence near the lighthouse. He appeared to be carrying a long rifle with a bayonet. They stopped and told a park ranger about him.

Chapter 20
Additional Southern Spirits

Only in Southern Maryland will you find a blue dog and a haunted witch-cursed rock—two of the oldest ghost stories in Maryland. The blue dog was unable to guard his master, but that hasn't stopped him from protecting his master's treasure for several hundred years. Moll Dyer died after being run out of town for being a witch. The rock where her body was found still bears the imprint of her hand and haunts Saint Mary's Historical Society, where it is located.

PEDDLER'S ROCK
Rose Hill Road, Port Tobacco, 20677

Maryland has the distinction of having the oldest ghost story: the blue dog. It dates back to the 1700s, although it wasn't written down until 1897. Many versions of the story exist, but most of the elements are very similar.

A peddler or soldier named Charles Thomas Sims had stopped at a tavern in Port Tobacco for a few drinks. As liquor is inclined to do, it loosened his lips and he bragged about having a good deal of gold plus the deed to an estate in his possession. Eventually, he and his dog, a large blue tick hound, left the tavern and headed out of town on Rose Hill Road.

Henry Hanos and possibly two accomplices followed Sims from the tavern. They attacked him and stole his money. During the attack, Sims and his dog were killed. Hanos then buried the loot under a holly tree along the road. The townspeople found Sims and his dog lying on a large rock, dead or nearly dead, the following day. You can still see reddish stains on the rock from their blood.

Hanos later returned to Rose Hill Road to retrieve his ill-gotten goods, but was scared away by the ghost of Sims's dog. Hanos then fell ill and died suddenly without ever retrieving the gold. From that day, the blue dog's ghost continues to guard his master's treasure.

Another version of the legend has the dog belonging to a former owner of Rose Hill, a mansion overlooking the Port Tobacco River. The man didn't trust banks and buried his money six feet from an old oak tree on the property. His dog is said to appear at midnight, wander the grounds, and then disappear.

One person who claimed to have seen the blue dog was Olivia Floyd, a former resident of Rose Hill. Olivia was an inimitable individual. She broke her back as a child, and because it was never set right she remained crippled. Despite this, she became a spy for the Confederation during the Civil War.

She used to tell a story about how the "Negroes" saw the blue dog come over the hill in a cloud of smoke the day her brother, Bob, died. Bob Floyd had been wounded at the Battle of Kelly's Ford as a member of J. E. B. Stuart's cavalry on March 17, 1863. He never recovered and passed on April 3, 1863. Olivia kept the bullet that killed Bob on the drawing room mantel.

To this day people report hearing the blue dog howling. Some even claim that the dog has chased them. Howling is usually heard on winter nights. If you want to see the dog, some claim he always makes an appearance on February 8, the day he and his master died. He is said to be very large and charcoal gray with a blue tint in color.

SAINT MARY'S HISTORICAL SOCIETY
41680 Tudor Place, Leonardtown, 20650

Moll Dyer was an eccentric recluse who lived on the edge of what was then Leonard Town in the late 1600s. At some point, the town's people decided she was a witch, and one cold winter's night they burned down her hut and drove her out of town. She was found several days later, frozen to death on a rock by the sea. When they removed her body, they found her hand and knee had left an impression on the rock.

The rock was moved in the 1970s to a spot in front of Saint Mary's Historical Society. Moving the rock was fraught with calamities that included several failed attempts and a broken crane, which led many to believe the rock was cursed. People report feeling ill-at-ease and even report aches and pains that occur when they stand near it. Many cameras also fail when people attempt to photograph the rock.

Those driving down Moll Dyer Road claim that she still haunts it. A white mist floats above the road that suddenly disappears. A phantom white dog has also been seen running up and down the road that seems to have some unknown connection to Moll Dyer.

SUMMERSEAT FARM
26655 THREE NOTCH ROAD, MECHANICSVILLE, 20659

Behind the main house of Summerseat Farm is a small cemetery with only a handful of graves. One grave is that of a Confederate soldier, Christopher Ireland Dorsey Costigan, who continues to haunt the cemetery. His ghost has been seen by several people. One reported that he appeared "headless." However, Christopher died with his head firmly attached to his body. He was wounded during Lee's retreat at Antietam at Philamount (he was with the First Maryland Regiment serving under Stonewall Jackson). The wound required his leg to be amputated. He died as a result of those wounds.

Christopher is just one of many ghosts who haunt the property. Most of the paranormal activity occurs in the house. Most of it is standard haunted-house stuff: a rosary hanging on a bedpost swings, sheets and blankets are pulled off of visitors as they sleep, objects move on their own, and lights turn on and off without cause.

Summerseat Farm dates back to June 1678, when the first tract of land was granted to Baker Brooke, although he died before getting the patent. A large Georgia-style house was built on the property in 1773. In the 1800s, the house was the family home of the Costigans, many of whom are buried in a family plot on the grounds. The original house was destroyed in a fire on March 11, 1874. Ten years later, in 1884, a new house was finally finished. The property was a family home until September 27, 2001, when it was sold to a nonprofit organization. It is currently a working farm.

At least two paranormal investigations have been done at the property. One was by Maryland Society of Ghost Hunters in 2009. They did not have any paranormal experiences during their investigation, until they went to leave. After turning off the lights and locking up, they noticed a light had been turned on in the parlor.

The second group was The Atlantic Paranormal Society (TAPS) for their television show *Ghost Hunters*. They heard footsteps walking on the floor above them several times, even though no one else was in the building. Christopher seemed to be very responsive. He managed to turn on a flashlight in the cemetery in response to questions and then formed a white mist near the bottom of a tree. They also saw several shadows that moved and made noises and had something run by the camera that had a bright light.

SOTTERLEY PLANTATION
44300 SOTTERLEY LANE, HOLLYWOOD, 20636

One should be wary of the ghost at Sotterley Plantation. He's been known to be a little aggressive when crossed. He's thrown rocks, punched a person in the arm, and even shoved one person down the stairs. But to be fair, he gets a little upset when people don't do what he wants them to in *his* house. The ghost is that of George Platter III, or at least he is one of the ghosts here.

Platter was born at Sotterley in 1735. His father had acquired the property a few years earlier. He was the one who gave it the name "Sotterley." He lived in the house until his death in 1792. The house then went to his son, George

Platter IV. But the son only outlived his father by ten years. After George IV died, the house was sold out of the Platter family to the Briscoes, who owned it in the 1800s. They sold it to Herbert Saterlee in 1910. The ghosts that haunt Sotterley are from the Platter and Briscoe families.

George III tends to stay on the second level of the estate. Volunteers are told not to go up to that area of the house, and with good reason. One volunteer who ignored the order and wandered up there found himself shoved down the stairs by unseen hands.

Another employee who had been hired to clean had left the vacuum on in one of the first-floor rooms and walked away. When she returned, it had been turned off. After this happened two more times, she told the ghost to stop bothering her and went outside for some fresh air. As she was outside, a rock flew past her head. Apparently the ghost was determined to get the last word.

Working at the plantation takes steel nerves. One employee was encompassed by a black mass while closing the mansion, another was punched in her right side while in a dark room alone, and a third repeatedly heard her name being called when no one else was around.

But not all the spirits are unpleasant. Sometimes the smell of coffee and bacon fills the air, even though nothing is being cooked. There are also the mandatory cold spots and lights being turned on and off that happen in every haunted house.

MAIDSTONE

CORNWALL ROAD AND CHESAPEAKE BENCH ROAD, OWINGS, 20736

On moonlit nights, a graceful lady strolls through the gardens at Maidstone wearing a long gray veil over what appears to be a wedding dress. They call her the "Gray Lady," and she has been haunting the house for over two hundred years.

Many believe the Gray Lady is Ann Chew Thomas. Ann married Philip Thomas in 1724 at Maidstone, which belonged to her father at the time. Records show that Ann went on to have six children before her death in 1771. No one knows what would cause her to return to her parents' house after her death. Samuel Chew, Ann's father, built the original house in the late 1600s. A stone house replaced the original one in the 1700s.

Ann haunts the house, although she has never been seen in the house. (One witness did see her leaving the house as he left the stables.) She often rearranges pictures on the walls. She even pushed one man off a couch as he was sleeping.

Part 6

WESTERN

Western Maryland is filled with mountains, forests, and small towns. It includes the counties of Washington, Allegany, and Garrett. Of the three counties, Garrett is remarkably ghostless. Although, considering the Civil War history of its neighbors, this shouldn't be too astonishing.

The bloodiest day of the Civil War, the Battle of Antietam, was fought here. About twenty-three thousand men were dead, wounded, or missing at the end of September 17, 1862. Not too surprising that such a tragic event has created a few ghosts.

Chapter 21
Antietam

The Battle of Antietam was the first major battle of the Civil War to be fought on Union soil and the bloodiest single-day battle in American history. By the time the suns set on September 17, 1862, close to twenty-three thousand Americans were dead, wounded, or missing. A tragedy of such proportion always creates a few ghosts, and Antietam is well-known for them.

PRY HOUSE FIELD HOSPITAL MUSEUM
18906 SHEPHERDSTOWN PIKE, KEEDYSVILLE, 21756

In 1976 a fire broke out in the Pry House. Firefighters fighting the blaze reported seeing a woman in a second-story window. They reported it to their captain, eager to go in and save the poor soul. Their captain informed them the family had all escaped safely. More important, the floor of that room had already collapsed; no one could have been standing there if he or she wanted to. The firefighters had seen the ghost of Mrs. Frances Richardson, a ghostly remnant from the Battle of Antietam.

During the Battle of Antietam, the Pry House was used as General George B. McClellan's headquarters. When another general, Israel Richardson, was wounded, he was given a room there to recover. His wound was slight, and his recovery seemed guaranteed. Unfortunately, infection set in and he passed away two months later. During that time, his wife had arrived. She tirelessly cared for him at Pry House until his death, which may be why her ghost lingers in the house.

After the fire the house sat empty for about a year before work began to restore it. Construction went slowly, because the National Park Service (NPS) had trouble keeping workers there. Crews would arrive to see a woman dressed in eighteenth-century dress standing in the window. But when they went in and discovered no floor to the room she was standing in, they would freak out and leave immediately.

But she's not always content with watching. According to Lori Eggleston in a 2013 article for the *Frederick News-Post*, the NPS had partnered with the National Museum of Civil War Medicine (NMCWM) to open a museum at the Pry House in 2005. George Wunderlich, executive director at the NMCWM, had arrived at Pry House to clear out some items inside for the exhibits. To make things easier, he opened all the doors in the house. As soon as he finished, all the doors slammed shut one by one, starting with the front door. It was as if someone was walking through the building and closing them.

Not to be deterred, Wunderlich opened them again. Again, as soon as he finished, the doors slammed shut one by one, but this time it started with the back door. April Dietrich was running an overnight program at the Pry House when she had a problem with the doors as well, or rather one door. According to her, she was "awakened around 1:30 a.m. to the sound of pacing on the front porch and a strange metallic scratching noise. When I opened my eyes, I realized that the key was turning in the lock. It was an old skeleton key that was difficult for me to turn as I had locked up hours before. I'm not sure whether the key was turning to let whoever was outside in, or to keep them out; but either way, I didn't want to know then."

Another employee, George, spent the night in the house and reported hearing "a loud banging noise from the front of the house." He ignored it at first, but then he heard several more "loud thumps and bangs." He told Eggleston, "I thought it sounded like someone was pacing back and forth along the hallway. This back-and-forth continued off and on for about an hour." These noises were followed by the sound of voices in conversation.

"Most of the voices sounded like they were coming from the formal parlor. I could definitely identify a male voice and at least two separate female voices, but could not discern anything they were saying." Rather than investigate or leave, George barricaded himself in the bedroom and waited for morning to come.

People have had doors slam and lock behind them, discovered lights on in the house after locking up and turning on the alarm, hearing footsteps on the stairs, and seeing lights move through the house after dark. But don't think you're safe from the ghosts outside. People report hearing voices and seeing strange lights inside the Pry Barn, too.

BLOODY LANE
5831 Dunker Church Road, Sharpsburg, 21782

The Battle of Antietam was fought on September 17, 1862, and is the bloodiest single-day battle in American history with 22,717 casualties, including 3,654 killed and 17,292 wounded. A sunken road between two farms saw the worst of the battle. In a few short hours, 5,600 men lay dead or wounded in the area now known as "Bloody Lane."

Seeing ghostly soldiers still engaging in battle is a common sight at almost every battlefield. Some feel that highly emotional events imprint themselves on a location, and when the time and circumstances are just right, the events replay themselves, like a natural tape recorder. Often people will see soldiers and assume they are reenactors, until the soldiers vanish in front of their eyes.

At Antietam, people have seen soldiers moving slowly and carefully around Bloody Lane as if they were stepping around bodies. One man reported that a group of Confederate soldiers walking down the road disappeared in front of him. Some report smelling gunpowder and smoke in the area. Other people have reported hearing gunshots, cannon blasts, and men's voices as if still in battle. Then there is the story of a group of seventh graders on a school trip.

One group that fought hard to capture Bloody Lane was the Sixty-ninth New York Militia. Also referred to as the Irish Brigade, they were known for their reckless bravery. At Antietam, they charged across 350 yards of terrain yelling their war cry, "Faugh-a-Ballagh," Gallic for "Clear the way!" By the end of the day, they had lost 60 percent of their men.

Years later, a group of students from McDonogh School had finished a trip to Antietam and were writing essays about their experiences. As their teacher went through them, he found a number of students had written about hearing Christmas carols being sung repeatedly. When he questioned the students, they reported they had heard someone chanting or singing the line from *Deck the Halls:* "Fa-la-la-la-lah." As the students had not seen anyone nearby, they assumed the sound was piped in from hidden speakers.

Their teacher, Mr. O'Brien, immediately asked them if what they heard was "Fah-ah-bah-lah"? The students agreed that was what they heard. Mr. O'Brien realized that they had heard the war cry from the Irish Brigade: Faugh-a-Ballagh.

BURNSIDE BRIDGE
BURNSIDE BRIDGE ROAD, SHARPSBURG, 21782

Burnside Bridge is another paranormal hotspot. The twelve-foot-wide stone bridge was known as Rohrback Bridge before General Ambrose Burnside pushed the Confederates back during the battle. Many of the men who died defending the bridge were buried in unmarked graves nearby. But that didn't stop Confederate sharpshooters from taking down a number of his soldiers first. Many of these men were buried in unmarked graves around the bridge. People report seeing balls of blue light floating around Burnside Bridge similar to the blue of a Union soldier's uniform. The lonely sound of a drum playing a single cadence also has been reported here.

OTTO/SHERRICK/PIPER HOUSES

Three other houses associated with Antietam are also haunted. Several park rangers have reported seeing a translucent, blue figure in the doorway of the Otto House. It appeared as if she was wearing a hoop skirt like a Southern belle. Just down the road is the Sherrick Farm, where people have also seen ghostly apparitions. Finally there is the Piper House, where a misty apparition is seen in an upstairs doorway and muffled voices are heard. Owners of the house were reluctant to admit its presence, but so many people have claimed to have experiences that they have had to reluctantly change their viewpoint.

ST. PAUL EPISCOPAL CHURCH
209 WEST MAIN STREET, SHARPSBURG, 21782

Like any town near a battlefield, every available building in Sharpsburg became a hospital or a morgue. This included St. Paul Episcopal Church, located on Main Street. Toward the end of the battle, Confederate troops retreated through the town, bringing the battle with them. The church was badly damaged as a result. People have heard screams and sobbing coming from within the church at night. Others report seeing lights flickering inside the church's tower. The church was rebuilt after the war, but stones from the original church were used.

ROSE HILL CEMETERY
600 SOUTH POTOMAC STREET, HAGERSTOWN, 21740

What could be spookier than a cemetery that contains a cemetery? Welcome to Rose Hill Cemetery.

In 1864 Washington County Senator Louis Firey submitted a proposal for the state to purchase twenty acres of Antietam Battlefield for the purpose of a state and national cemetery. Up until that point "the bodies of our heroes who fell in that great struggle" were "bleaching in the upturned furrows." It wasn't that they had not been buried, but rather they were buried hastily in shallow graves. Erosion and animals had exposed many of the graves, leaving the bodies exposed. Keep in mind Union soldiers buried everyone after the battles of South Mountain and Antietam. They took more care with Union dead than they did Confederate dead.

Firey's proposal died. A cemetery at Antietam was eventually established, but only Union soldiers were buried there. In 1866, Rose Hill Cemetery was established and a movement to create a cemetery within Rose Hill for Confederate soldiers began. Eventually, Washington Cemetery was established for this purpose. In 1872 the first Confederate soldiers were moved from Antietam and reinterred. A total of 2,468 Confederate soldiers are now buried at Washington, including those originally buried in Daniel Wise's well (see chapter 13). Only 281 are identified.

Many of the soldiers had been buried without markers. The few markers that had been placed were often faded or had disappeared in the ten years since their burial. The lack of a decent marker combined with their reburial may be why their spirits have not found rest. People have reported seeing soldiers within the cemetery. It is such a popular tale that it is mentioned on Maryland Historical Trust's Inventory of Historic Properties form.

Another ghost in the cemetery is a widow. She is dressed in black and is often heard weeping. The best place to spot her is near her husband's grave, but no one is sure which grave it is. If you try to approach her and ask, she is said to vanish.

A final legend says if you drive to the back of the cemetery in front of the crematorium and turn your engine off, you will hear the sound of someone screaming for help and detect the scent of "burnt hair." One major problem with this story: There is no crematorium in the cemetery. (Author's note: My guess is a peacock either lives nearby or got into the cemetery at one point. They make a sound that is often mistaken for someone calling for help.)

Chapter 22
Other Western Wisps

Outside of Antietam, Western Maryland has a number of other ghosts. This region appears to be less haunted in comparison to the rest of the state. Perhaps it is just that Antietam overshadows the rest of the stories. Interestingly, only one of the ghosts here has any connection to the Civil War.

CHURCH OF ST. PATRICK
201 North Centre Street, Cumberland, 21502

Father Edward Brennan was born in April 1827, in Kildare, Ireland. He went to St. Mary's Seminary at Baltimore and was ordained in 1858. One month later he was made the pastor of St. Patrick's Church in Cumberland, a job he kept until his death in 1884. Father Brennan had a number of troubling experiences during the Civil War, but one was particularly troubling.

He was called to minister a young soldier before his execution. Private Francis "Frank" Gillespie had no history of undisciplined behavior when he took out a revolver and shot Lieutenant William B. Shearer in the face. At his court-martial, evidence came out that Shearer had ordered Gillespie to be "hung by his thumbs" for breaking army regulations. The punishment was extremely painful and almost killed Gillespie. He vowed to get revenge, which he did on July 7, 1864.

Gillespie was hanged near Rose Hill Cemetery in Cumberland. Before he died, he trusted some tokens of affection to Father Brennan. Brennan was going to ensure that they made it back to Gillespie's wife in New York. Father Brennan promised him that he would take care of it. According to Father Brennan, shortly after Gillespie's execution on July 11, 1864, he was in his room alone when he heard heavy footsteps coming down the hall followed by a knock on his door. He opened the door to find the ghost of Frank Gillespie, who chastised him for being slow to keep his promise.

This story has long been told by parishioners of St. Patrick's Church. Remarkably, many of the facts of the story check out. A letter to the editor of the *Syracuse Journal* was sent July 8, 1864, as a tribute to Shearer after his "homicide" on the march between Parkersburg, West Virginia, and Cumberland. In the cemetery of St. Patrick's Church are the graves of both Father Brennan and Francis Gillespie. Records show that Gillespie was hanged for murder.

PUCCINI RESTAURANT
12901 ALI GHAN ROAD NORTHEAST, CUMBERLAND, 21502

Employees at Puccini Restaurant know that when they go into the basement alone to retrieve a pizza, they won't return alone. A second set of footsteps will be heard walking behind them, but when they look, no one will be there. Sometimes they hear someone whispering behind them or just feel another presence with them in the basement.

The house that houses the restaurant has been standing for over two hundred years. During the Civil War it had a front-row seat to the Battle of Flock's Mill and was used as a hospital. The attic still bears engravings believed to be done by soldiers during that time. But no one knows the identity of the ghosts haunting it.

In the main dining room, employees often report seeing objects move on their own. Bottles and glasses frequently fall off perfectly level shelves and a faucet turns itself on. A prep cook who works early mornings reported seeing shadows gliding past him out of the corner of his eye, even though no one else is in the building.

Paul Burch, a co-manager of the restaurant, had an experience the first night he had to close by himself.

"I was in the office and I kept hearing [chairs scraping across the floor and footsteps]," he told the *Cumberland Times-News* in 2010. "I mean, I was getting up out of my chair and coming out to see what was going on, and it would be quiet."

A little girl also haunts the place. She is believed to have died in one of the second-floor rooms after she fell near the fireplace and her dress caught fire. She was seen standing in the hallway of the first floor. In a 2010 investigation, City Lights Paranormal attempted to make contact with the little girl by hanging a set of keys in the hallway. They reported hearing the keys jingle when no one was in the room and seeing them sway back and forth.

MARYLAND THEATRE
27 South Potomac Street, Hagerstown, 21740

Workaholics aren't limited to the living. The Maryland Theatre is haunted by one of its first managers who worked there in the 1930s until the 1960s. The identity of the ghost was confirmed by the manager's daughter, who claims to have seen him at the theater. Staff members can't deny that they often feel as if someone unseen is with them.

A cleaning lady was working in the upper balcony in 2013 when she heard her name, Sharon. She paused, looked around, but didn't see anyone. She chalked it up to her imagination and went back to work, until she heard her name again. As no one else was nearby, she had no other explanation but the ghost.

Another employee was terrified after seeing a white, translucent figure in the boiler room. The employee thought he'd be able to sneak a cigarette there, but the ghost thought otherwise. And the ghost has reason to be protective of the theater. In 1974 a fire broke out in the theater. It destroyed the lobby and apartments above it, but stopped at the doors to the main theater.

Michael Harsh, a former executive director of the theater, feels the ghost is protective of the theater and never felt uncomfortable there. One poster on the Internet was not so lucky. He claims he was in the theater with friends when they felt hands on their backs pushing them, followed by a voice telling them to "Get out." It seems the manager didn't think they needed to be in the theater.

The Maryland Theatre opened in 1915 as a vaudeville and movie house. Today it houses cultural events and premier performances.

OLD SOUTH MOUNTAIN INN
6132 OLD NATIONAL PIKE, BOONSBORO, 21713

In 2009 a guest at Old South Mountain Inn approached a server to ask who the woman at the top of the stairs in front of the dining room was. He had seen a woman walking back and forth. The server had no idea who he could be referring to until the guest mentioned that the woman was wearing a blue velvet dress. It was a former owner of the inn, Madeline Dahlgren. In every picture of her, she is wearing a blue velvet dress.

Old South Mountain Inn is old. It dates back to 1732. Being that old means it has seen a lot of history, including several presidents who have stayed at the inn. Dahlgren bought the inn in 1876 and used it as a private residence until her death in 1898. Apparently she decided she liked it so much, she didn't want to leave, which has proven lucky for the current owners.

One night one of the maintenance staff had stayed late to wait for a delivery. As he was puttering around killing time, he noticed that a door that was always closed and locked had been opened. He moved to close the door when he smelled smoke. The rear of the inn was on fire. He immediately called the fire department and the building was saved. Many believe that Dahlgren's ghost opened the door to bring the fire to his attention.

One of the current co-owners, Chad Dorsey, had his own experience shortly after taking over the inn that he told to the *Frederick News-Post* in 2009.

"It was the middle of the day. [My dog] Sonny was laying on the floor in front of my desk and he's looking over my right shoulder, with the fur raised up on his neck and his tail wagging," Dorsey said. He looked around but didn't see anyone, but he did sense something. "I felt a presence behind me," Dorsey said. "I just sensed someone was behind me." No one else was there.

People also report seeing doors shake as if someone is trying to get in and hearing voices and footsteps in empty rooms of the house. These may not all be attributed to Dahlgren, as ghostly soldiers have been seen. In 1862 General D. H. Hill used the inn as his headquarters during the Battle of South Mountain.

JONATHAN HAGER HOUSE
110 KEY STREET, HAGERSTOWN, 21740

Jonathan Hager purchased two hundred acres of land in 1739, which he called "Hager's Fancy." He immediately began building a house on the property. The location for the three-and-a-half-story house was carefully placed over a spring and had walls twenty-two inches thick. The protected water supply and impregnable walls allowed the house to double as a fortress, necessary in the 1700s when the threat of Indian attacks was high.

Those that haunt the house are not Jonathan Hager or his relatives. He sold the house to Jacob Rohrer in 1745.

Michael Hammond purchased it in 1813. It was later purchased by the Downins in the latter part of the 1800s. The house eventually became the property of the City of Hagerstown. The house was carefully restored to its colonial glory by the Washington County Historical Society. It was opened to the public in 1962.

Many believe it is the ghosts of the Hammonds and Downins that haunt the place. Through the years at least thirteen people have died in the house (although we all know that you don't have to die somewhere to come back to haunt it).

Children of the Downin family are believed to pull a variety of haunting tricks on guests to Hager House. They frequently move a corncob doll to different locations in the house and have been heard running up the stairs and giggling. They may also be the reason that lightbulbs, cameras, and batteries frequently fail inside the house. A man dressed in black is seen walking on the back porch of the house. He's been known to pause and enjoy a pipe on occasion. A rocking chair likes to rock all by itself. Voices are frequently heard, as are screams coming from the basement.

According to John Bryan, historic sites facilitator, most people report seeing a young woman dressed in nineteenth-century clothing. She's been seen in the upper hallway and on the second-floor staircase. A guide was giving a tour when she spotted the woman wearing a green dress passing through one of the rooms.

Bryan had his own experience that he related in *Mysteries and Lore of Western Maryland*. "I felt what I can only describe as a 'poke in the back'; it was strange, the feeling of coldness and like that spot went to sleep, only a moment."

He felt a similar poke a few minutes later, but again no one was around him.

Smells without a discernable source have also been reported. Sometimes it is the smell of cherry pie, while other times it is the smell of pipe tobacco.

Part 7

EASTERN SHORE

The Eastern Shore has some of the oldest ghost stories connected with it and some extremely haunted towns. The Eastern Shore is the part of Maryland that lies east of the Chesapeake Bay and west of the Atlantic Ocean and Delaware. The area is divided into nine counties: Caroline, Cecil, Dorchester, Kent, Queen Anne's, Somerset, Talbot, Wicomico, and Worcester. The area is mostly rural—only 8 percent of the population of Maryland lives in the area—and it's dotted with friendly fishing villages.

Chapter 23
Eastern Legends

Baltimore's Eastern Shore is host to several legends, including four ghostly ones. The first two ghosts are Patty Cannon and Kitty Knight. While the two women lived around the same time in American history, they could not be more different. The third story tells of a darker moment in Maryland's history with a villain who is extremely stubborn. Sadly, the story of the sea monster Chessie won't be covered here. Although, maybe she's actually the ghost of a dinosaur...

PATTY CANNON'S HOUSE

Finchville Reliance Road at Reliance Road, Federalsburg, 21632

In the spring of 1829, a tenant farmer was clearing some brush when his horse sunk into a grave. He uncovered a body. According to newspaper reports at the time, the body belonged to a man who had disappeared (along with the fifteen thousand dollars he had on him) while on his way to buy slaves. A search of the property uncovered more bodies, including those of several children.

For years Patty Cannon and her son-in-law, Joe Johnson, had been kidnapping free black men and women and selling them into slavery. In 1807 Congress passed the Act Prohibiting Importation of Slaves, which went into effect on

January 1, 1808. The act banned importation of slaves into the United States. While it might be viewed as an action designed to abolish slavery, several Southern congressmen voted for it, believing that the current slave population (around four million in 1807) would sustain itself.

While the 1807 act carried stiff fines, it wasn't until an additional act was passed in 1820 that the importation of slaves sharply declined. The new act carried the possibility of death for anyone found participating in the crime. Patty Cannon decided to profit over this change. Rather than import new slaves, she would kidnap free blacks and sell them into slavery.

In 1822 she and Johnson were indicted for the crime, but only Johnson was tried. The sentence wasn't death, but instead one hour in the pillory and thirty-nine lashes. Cannon built her house on the border of Maryland and Delaware. According to legend, when someone from Maryland came to arrest her, she walked over to Delaware and vice versa if someone came from Delaware.

Cannon committed suicide in jail on May 11, 1829. It is unknown how many men, women, and children she sold into slavery or how many people she killed. Usually the ghosts of people who were wronged or suffered come back to haunt. But thankfully their spirits have found peace. Perhaps it is karma that Patty Cannon hasn't.

According to a report published in the *Philadelphia Times* on March 24, 1879, that "Johnson's Cross-roads, Sussex, has been frightened out of its wits by the appearance in the streets of the village of the ghost of Patty Cannon, the negro-stealer of bygone days." (Johnson's Crossroads became Reliance in 1882 and is now considered part of Federalsburg.) The account sadly lacks details about the haunting, but legend says Patty's ghost wandered the back roads, sometimes alone, other times leading a line of chained, wailing victims toward the state line.

Cannon's ghost has also been reported at both her house and Joe Johnson's tavern, which was very close to her house. Both are believed to be places where Cannon and Johnson kidnapped, enslaved, and occasionally murdered free blacks.

A historical marker put up in 1939 says, "Nearby Stood Patty Cannon's House." The "Nearby Stood" was added after an episode of *History's Detectives* proved the house behind the sign was too young to be Cannon's house. Cannon's house, which had been closer to the Maryland–Delaware state line, was demolished in 1948.

People visiting the site have reported seeing the ghost of a "hideous old woman" and hearing people crying (which they insist are from the ghosts of the people she tortured to death).

Joe Johnson's tavern is also supposed to be haunted. In 1885 the building was heavily reworked until it bore no resemblance to the original tavern. It was located on the northwest corner, likely where a florist is today. Whether or not that building contains some of the original structure or if the tavern was demolished in the past is unclear.

Former owners of the tavern claimed that Patty Cannon's spirit would prowl through the building the minute the sun went down. Additional tortured cries were also said to be heard coming from that building. Doors would open by themselves and heavy footsteps were heard.

KITTY KNIGHT HOUSE
14028 AUGUSTINE HERMAN HIGHWAY, GEORGETOWN, 21930

When you stay in Room 4 of the Historic Kitty Knight House, leave the door open when you enter. If the door closes behind you, then you've been welcomed by the resident ghost. If it doesn't . . . well, you might want to request another room.

In March 1813 Rear Admiral George Cockburn started the "Chesapeake Campaign" in which the British Royal Navy raided American towns and properties along the coast of the Chesapeake Bay and its rivers. The campaign continued until the Battle of Baltimore, September 12–14, 1814.

On May 6, 1813, the British sailed toward the towns of Georgetown and Fredericktown intent on raiding them for valuable supplies. They sent word that if they surrendered peacefully, their homes would not be burned and all lost property would be paid for. But Kent County had four hundred men ready and waiting to face them. When the militia failed to kill many of the British soldiers, they retreated. As a result, the British burned several of the houses and businesses and most of the townspeople fled. Kitty Knight stayed.

Catharine "Kitty" Knight had taken refuge in one of two brick houses near the Sassafras River. When the British pounded on the door and told her to leave as they set fire to it, Kitty extinguished the fires while pleading with them to spare the house along with its neighbor house. It wasn't even her house (although she did purchase it later).

She managed to convince the British not to burn the houses. Some say it was her beauty that did the trick; others say it was her spirit that won over the British. And while her beauty is legendary, it is her spirit that lives on in the house that now bears her name.

Room 4 is believed to be Kitty's former bedroom. A rocking chair belonging to Kitty used to be in the room. The staff removed it after too many guests complained about it rocking on its own. Employees receive calls from the room, but no one is on the line. They immediately check the room to ensure a guest is not in trouble, only to discover it is unoccupied.

But Kitty doesn't keep to her bedroom. She is dressed in nineteenth-century clothing walking down the staircase. A shadowy form, also believed to be Kitty, is seen in the dining area. Kitty can be a bit of a prankster. She often turns on lights in unoccupied rooms. Staff members who notice them (because they are outside on their way home) are forced to go to the room to turn them off, only to discover that Kitty has already done it for them.

THE CAROLINE COUNTY DEPARTMENT OF CORRECTIONS
101 GAY STREET, DENTON, 21629

According to the July 17, 1915, *Denton Journal*, fifteen-year-old Mildred Clark was going through a strip of woods near Federalsburg to visit her aunt when she was attacked by a "negro." The girl later identified her attacker as nineteen-year-old Aloysius "Wish" Sheppard, who (according to the article) confessed to the crime to the sheriff after he was arrested.

The trial took place over two days. Sheppard took the stand and denied having made a confession or committing the crime. It didn't really matter if he was guilty or not. Sheppard had been in trouble with the law before and indicted at least once for stealing. And he was a black man in the South who was accused of attacking a white girl. That was enough for him to hang—one way or the other.

While a lynch mob was ready to act, they didn't need to. The judge found Sheppard guilty, and he was sentenced to death. An estimated one thousand people witnessed his hanging on August 27, 1915. Afterward, the rope was cut into small pieces for people to take home as "souvenirs."

According to legend, Sheppard did not go to the gallows peacefully. When they came to take him, he clung to the bars and cell walls in a futile effort to prevent his death. When the sheriff returned to the cell after the hanging, he found a handprint on the wall. He scrubbed and scrubbed to remove it, but it didn't budge. Other sheriffs tried to paint over it through the years, but it kept returning, until they finally installed a new wall in front of it.

In a 2013 article by Mindie Burgoyne for *What's Up?* magazine, Burgoyne interviewed Louis Andrews, who lived in a house attached to the jail when his father was sheriff. He recalls seeing and even trying to remove the handprint (unsuccessfully) from the jail. He also told of inmates who complained of hearing footsteps or chains clanking up the steel steps and seeing Sheppard in the hall late at night. Sometimes he would be nothing more than a shadow; other times his red eyes would glow at them.

One inmate claimed the scratches on his body were due to a struggle he had with the ghost. Other inmates complained their watches were ripped off their arms. The watches were later found broken in the jailyard. Then there was the door to his cell. It refused to open without a struggle.

After the renovations, Sheppard moved his hauntings from the prisoners to the staff. Employees watched the empty elevator ride between floors, saw locked file cabinets open or slam shut, and also saw Sheppard's red eyes glaring at them through windows and doors.

Interestingly, the account of his hanging does not mention anything about Sheppard being anxious or reluctant. In fact it says exactly the opposite, that he "slept soundly" the night before but "awoke early, still indifferent and careless of his quick-coming doom." So, it may not be fear that left his handprint or keeps his spirit in the jail.

BLACKWATER NATIONAL WILDLIFE REFUGE
2145 Key Wallace Drive, Cambridge, 21613

Blackwater National Wildlife Refuge offers twenty-seven thousand acres of freshwater ponds, tidal marshes, and tree-laden forests; thousands of migrating ducks and geese; and one demonic, ghostly mule. The mule was a problem at some point before 1933, when the refuge was created. It was known to attack fishers and loggers. Local residents decided it wasn't mean or rabid, it was demonic. They lured it to a patch of quicksand, where it was swallowed up and died.

But the mule wasn't done terrorizing people. People report seeing it in the marshy areas and claim it is trying to lure—or drive—them toward quicksand so they suffer a similar fate. Those who see it claim it has red glowing eyes. Some state they have heard it snorting or feel its hot breath on the back of their necks.

Chapter 24
Easton

Easton's website proudly declares that it is the "Eighth Best Small Town in America," although they don't explain why. (Norman Crampton placed them eighth in his 1996 book The 100 Best Small Towns in America.*) If you based how good a town is on the number of ghosts it has, then Easton would definitely place in the top 100. It has a surprising number of ghosts for a town of a mere sixteen thousand people.*

TIDEWATER INN
101 East Dover Street, Easton, 21601

Downtown Easton looks exactly like one imagines the center of a small town to look like. The tree-lined streets contain a mixture of wood and brick buildings. One of the largest buildings found in the heart of downtown is the Tidewater Inn.

Arthur Johnson Grymes (sometimes known as A. J. or A. Johnson) put his heart and soul into building and managing the Tidewater Inn. He built the hotel in 1948, four years after the old hotel had burned to the ground. Construction was delayed by a shortage of materials during World War II.

Grymes died on April 18, 1963. According to his obituary, he managed the hotel until his death. The obituary was wrong though, since he seems to still be on the job. A security guard, Walter, working the nightshift, felt someone tug on his pant leg if it seemed he might be dozing off. Another night, Walter saw a face in a portal window on the door between the kitchen and the dining room. But when he checked, no one was in the dining room—plus the window was seven feet off the ground, so it would be difficult for anyone to quickly peek in and leave.

Employees on the top floor have also seen Grymes. However, this is not surprising because the space used to be his office. Doors have been heard slamming and people claim to hear their name being called, even though no one is around. Tidewater Inn doesn't mind having Mr. Grymes around; they even mention him on their website.

AVALON THEATRE
40 East Dover Street, Easton, 21601

Just down the street from the Tidewater Inn, is the Avalon Theatre, which contains two different ghosts. One ghost likes to ride the elevator, while the other throws knives at the Avalon Theater. Originally known as the "New Theatre" when it opened in 1921, the name changed when it was renovated in 1934 to a cinema. The Avalon eventually fell into disrepair and closed in 1985. Then in 1989, it was renovated a second time and opened as a performing arts center.

A vaudeville actress named Marguerite likes to ride the elevator at the Avalon. The elevator doors often open, and the car moves to the second and third floors without anyone pushing its buttons. She has also dropped the stage's fire curtain suddenly. A former owner of the Avalon claims he and another employee saw her one night. She stepped off the elevator then turned and dissolved through the doors leading into the theater.

According to the website Chesapeake Ghost Walks, Helen Chappell saw a ghost when she was rehearsing for a play. While onstage, she repeatedly saw someone in the balcony who disappeared whenever she tried to get a better look. Chappell also said the ghost haunted the landing behind the stage that leads to the Green Room in the basement.

A picture of Marguerite and several other Vaudeville actors appears in the lobby. Rumor has it she was murdered and her body left in the elevator, however no historical record of this event appeared in newspapers at the time.

Another ghost stays on the third floor of the building, which now houses a bar. Only one story has been shared about him. Apparently, one night two employees were cleaning up in the bar when they saw knives fly across the room. One was so shaken up that she left immediately and refused to return, not even to collect her paycheck.

ODD FELLOWS HALL
1 South Washington Street, Easton, 21601

Two blocks west of the Avalon, at the corner of Washington and Dover Streets is what was once the Odd Fellows Hall. Odd Fellows Hall was built in the mid-1800s as a meeting place for the International Fraternity of Odd Fellows. It currently houses a store with offices on the second and third floors. When they first moved in, tenants complained about the elevator moving on its own at all times of the day and night. The landlord called an engineer, who couldn't find anything wrong with it, and the problem was never resolved. Store employees also report being "touched" by unseen hands, having items moved on them, or being bumped even though no one is close to them.

OLD EASTON EMERGENCY HOSPITAL
7 SOUTH WASHINGTON STREET, EASTON, 21601

Next door to Odd Fellows is the Old Easton Emergency Hospital, which has been converted into retail and office spaces. Tenants also report hearing the elevator running on its own, followed by footsteps on the third floor. They would check to see who was there, only to discover they were alone and the offices locked. Odd that one town would have three ghosts that ride the elevator. But maybe Marguerite likes to moonlight.

TALBOT COUNTY COURTHOUSE
11 NORTH WASHINGTON STREET, EASTON, 21601

Slightly north of Dover is Talbot County Courthouse, whose ghost is a Peeping Tom. The Talbot County Courthouse employees call their ghost "the Colonel." He walks the halls at night. He also likes to unlock doors and peek in on people. Considering this behavior, it's not a big surprise that people report feeling like they are being watched. In the basement, he flushes the toilets and slams doors. Many believe that he is the ghost of Colonel Oswald Tilghman, who as a lawyer would have done business in the building when he was alive.

OLD EASTON JAIL

Corner of Federal and South West Streets, Easton, 21601

If you stay on Washington and turn on Federal Street, a block down you'll come to where the Old Easton Jail once stood. Any building that used to be a jail is likely to have some bad energy, which is the case for the old jail, which is now the office for Talbot County's state's attorney. When it was a jail, it housed both male and female prisoners along with the sheriff and his family. The sheriff was responsible for caring for prisoners until they went to court.

One day staff members working on the second floor noticed a man wearing a jacket and dark pants in front of the elevator. Since it is a secured federal building, they were confused who the man was, as no one had entered through the public entrance. One of them walked around the corner to investigate, but the man had vanished. Others have seen a woman dressed in blue standing near the elevators. Like the man, she vanishes without a trace.

ELSEWHERE IN EASTON

Just outside downtown Easton, at 24 North Aurora Street, is the **Foxley House**. According to the website Chesapeake Ghost Walks, it is the "Most Haunted House in Easton." It was once owned by Colonel Oswald Tilghman, great-grandson of Lieutenant Colonel Tench Tilghman. Census records show that an elderly woman lived with Tilghman's family for over ten years. Some believe she was mentally disturbed and the family kept her confined in the attic. She is now heard screaming. Strange, smoky shapes; unexplained lights; and even faces are seen in the upper windows of the house. Candles are also said to move around the house by themselves. Finally, mist and fog often manifest in the kitchen and living room.

North of Easton, on the peninsula between Gross and Lloyd Creeks, is another haunted Tilghman home: **Gross's Coate.** Late at night the ghost of Molly Tilghman is seen gliding down the stairway to unlock the front door. Her rebellious young nephew lived with her and was known to stay out late. His aunt refused to give him a key, however, and was forced to go down every night to let him in. Gross's Coate is located at 11300 Gross Coate Road.

Also north of Easton is what was once the **All Saints' Church.** All Saints' Church was built at the turn of the twentieth century just north of Easton. It has been transformed into a private home, because who wouldn't want to live in a haunted church with its own graveyard? Before the change, people reported hearing the organ play on its own and hearing screams from the bell tower and seeing ghosts sitting in the pews as if they were worshipping. The current owner has more trouble outside than in. His dog likes to bark at the grave of Willie J. Willis, a three-year-old who died in 1884. He also says that anyone who parks their car on top of Nettie Beaven's grave ends up having car trouble. The church is located at 10706 Longwoods Road.

Chapter 25
Lower Eastern Shore

The Lower Eastern Shore includes Worcester, Somerset, and Wicomico Counties and two haunted Atlantic Hotels. Many travel here to the resort town of Ocean City; others come to explore some of the haunted locations. The Atlantic Hotel in Berlin has a number of ghostly guests who refuse to check out. Meanwhile the one in Ocean City has a manager who refuses to go off duty. Then there is the six-fingered captain who murdered his unfaithful wife and the student who returned home to haunt after committing suicide.

ATLANTIC HOTEL (BERLIN)
2 NORTH MAIN STREET, BERLIN, 21811

A little girl haunts the second floor of the Atlantic Hotel in Berlin. Guests and staff have heard a child laughing, even though no children are staying in the hotel. They also have heard the sound of a ball bouncing down the hall and that of a tricycle being ridden.

Several rooms also have ghostly issues. Room 18's door closes on its own. Housekeeping tries to leave it open while they work, but when they are about to leave, the door slams in their face. The general manager had an interesting encounter in the room next door. A woman stepped out of Room 16 and complained she had no towels in her room. The general manager immediately got fresh towels and brought them to the room. But no one answered when she knocked. She opened the door and called out, but still no one answered. Finally, she went in, but the room showed no signs of anyone occupying the room. More significant was that the room was fully stocked with towels. Perplexed, she checked to see who had rented the room for the night, only to discover the room was unoccupied.

Staffers reported a strange smell in Room 16 during renovations. No matter how much they cleaned, the smell persisted. While changing the paper in the dresser drawers, they discovered a silhouette of George Washington, which they propped on the dresser. The following week, they were in Room 17 installing hair dryers when they found a second portrait, this one of a little girl.

The general manager decided to swap the Washington portrait with this new one, but when she got to Room 16, the portrait was missing. She looked around and discovered it hanging on the wall. No other pictures had been hung in the hotel and no one admitted to doing it. The hotel didn't even have the supplies to hang pictures yet.

Mindie Burgoyne relates a story about Room 24 on her blog *Who Cares What I Think?* According to a maintenance worker she talked to, while he was working in the room his paint scraper disappeared. He looked all over the room, but it was gone. He told her, "I had to go back to the shop to get a new one. When I came back to the room, there was my paint scraper standing straight up on its end in the middle of the room." He refused to work in that room after that.

Burgoyne also had her own experience in Room 23. She had run upstairs after checking in to change her clothes and freshen up. "When I came into the room, I had bags in both hands. I remember letting the door slam behind me. When I was ready to go downstairs, I noticed the security bar (the one found on the guest side of the hotel room door that you flip over as a security lock) had been moved to the 'locked' position. I found this odd because I knew I didn't lock my door, in fact I couldn't have because my hands were full. There was no one else in the room but me. How could it have gotten locked?"

The front desk has its own issues. Several lamps switch off when employees walk by them, only to turn back on later. The hotel tried changing the bulbs and checked the wiring, but it still happens. No one can explain it.

ATLANTIC HOTEL (OCEAN CITY)
401 SOUTH BALTIMORE AVENUE, OCEAN CITY, 21842

About ten miles down Highway 50 in Ocean City stands another haunted Atlantic Hotel. Dr. Charles Purnell bought the hotel in 1923. Two years later a fire devastated the building. Purnell rebuilt the hotel and spent the next forty years running it, until his death in 1962. So is it any wonder that he doesn't want to leave the hotel that he so loved during his life?

People have reported seeing a tall, thin man with thinning hair and round glasses wearing a suit. He has been seen in mirrors, walking along hallways, standing in corners, and looking out a window. Everyone who sees him claims he looks real until he vanishes before their eyes or walks through a closed door.

CELLAR HOUSE FARM
Cellar House Road, Pocomoke, 21851

Not much is known about Cellar House, except that it was built in the 1730s. Legend says a tunnel once connected the house to the riverbank. The tunnel allowed former residents to smuggle goods. The cellar tunnel likely gave the house its name and its ghosts.

One of the residents of Cellar House was a six-fingered sea captain who was gone long periods of time. After returning from one extended absence, he found his wife pregnant. After doing the math, he realized there was no way he could be the father. He threw her out of the house and told her never to return.

Months later the wife decided to return to her husband and beg his forgiveness. But on the way, her raft overturned and the baby drowned. She swam to shore and made it back to Cellar House. The sea captain had not forgiven her. When he saw her, he became enraged. He dragged her up to the master bedroom and stabbed her to death. Realizing that he'd be hanged for the crime, he left the house immediately and never returned. The floor is said to still bear the imprint of where the body lay rotting for several weeks. According to current owners, the bedroom does contain newer floorboards that suggest someone replaced them in the past.

Today, people report hearing a baby crying and a woman wailing in the swamp near Cellar House. A strange light has also been witnessed, believed to be the mother carrying a lantern and looking for her lost child. Urban legend says that if you park your car in the woods near Cellar House, you will find a strange six-fingered handprint on them. It is the captain warning you away. He may also be trying to protect the chests of loot that he hid on the property.

Today Cellar House is a private home, although the owners promote the ghost stories on their website devoted to the property.

RACKLIFFE HOUSE
11700 Tom Patton Lane, Berlin, 21811

Denise Milko was seventeen years old when she moved into the Rackliffe House with her aunt and cousin in 1968. According to Milko, "The very first night we were in the house we heard the distinct sound of a child crying. Not an infant but more like a toddler; we all heard it. Some tried to dismiss it as the barking of puppy frogs, but we knew what they sounded like, and it wasn't that. It was sobbing, and that was something that occurred all year long."

Unfortunately for Milko, she chose the most haunted room in the house to make into her bedroom. "Many nights, no one could sleep because there were so many bangs and thumps coming from my room. Of course, there was nothing going on. My aunt would say it sounded like I was housecleaning."

Some nights Milko awoke when a cold breeze moved over her and she would smell perfume in the air. Eventually, Milko moved out of that room in order to get some peace and quiet. But the hauntings weren't restrained to her room.

Milko frequently heard an older woman calling her name, even though she was alone. Her cousin Jeff heard a loud crash while alone in the house. But when he investigated, nothing had been disturbed. He refused to stay in the house alone after that. The family also heard the piano playing by itself and the sound of soft footsteps.

One night Denise was in the house alone when she heard dogs barking outside, followed by gunshots and the sound of glass breaking. She immediately called her father, who arrived with the sheriff. They searched the house, but found nothing, not even broken glass.

During a dinner party in the house, guest Gene Parker admitted that he didn't believe in ghosts. Suddenly the lights in the house turned off and the flames on the candles grew until they were six to eight inches high. A moment later, the lights turned back on and everyone witnessed Gene stabbing at the air in front of him with a letter opener.

Milko's family moved out in 1972, and the Whitlocks moved in. The ghosts stayed put. A few days after moving in, the Whitlocks returned home and found their dog outside. He had smashed through an antique window on the first floor to get out of the house.

Twenty years after moving out, Denise returned to her old home during an open house in 1992. The house seemed peaceful until she got to her old bedroom. On the floor a pile of *National Geographic* magazines had been laid out on the floor to spell the words "Go away."

DR. JOHN S. AYDELOTTE HOUSE
104 EAST MARKET STREET, SNOW HILL, 21863

Dr. John S. Aydelotte had two children: a son, William, and a daughter, Mildred. In 1904 William was a third-year pharmacy student attending the University of Maryland. He was staying in a boardinghouse on West Franklin Street in Baltimore.

On the morning of December 17, the owner of the board-inghouse heard a thud followed by groans. She opened the door and found William rolling on the floor with several deep gashes on his throat. He was taken to a hospital where he died.

The papers reported the next day that William had committed suicide "owing to an attack of melancholia caused by a recent illness and his inability to be graduated with his class." William had contracted tonsillitis and missed too much school. The papers also reported that William had been in contact with a young woman for several years and that they were to be married following his graduation in the spring.

William's family refused to believe he had committed suicide. Not only did he have three gashes on his throat, but the razor he used was found closed neatly on his bed. On the desk was an unfinished note to his father that read, "Dear Papa, it is useless to keep me at school . . ." While some took this as an unfinished suicide note, his family thought it meant he wanted to return home.

And despite his death, William appears to have followed up on his plans after he died. Many believe his spirit haunts the house where he grew up. Most of the paranormal experiences were reported in the 1990s when the property was a bed-and-breakfast known as the Snow Hill Inn.

In a 1993 article for the *Baltimore Sun*, owner Jim Washington said, "Some gentlemen were working on the house once, and there was a window that they couldn't open. It was painted shut or something. Then, one day when they were in the room, the window suddenly flew open. After that, they wouldn't stay in the house. They had been staying here while doing the work, and said the owners would have to get them hotel rooms somewhere else. These were grown construction men."

Washington also talked about how the smoke alarm went off without cause when he was by himself one afternoon. While he believed the ghost was William, he liked to call him "J. J." Whenever something happened, like the lights flickering, Washington would just tell people "Oh, that's just J. J."

Several guest reported seeing William's ghost. Margaret Mead was staying in the hotel with her fourteen-year-old son, Brandon. While Brandon was in the bathroom, he got a feeling like someone was watching him. He turned around and saw a "younger guy, dark-haired, pale and greenish" looking at him through the window.

Another woman was staying in the inn in 1992 when she saw the ghost. She awoke in the middle of the night to see a man walking around her bed toward the bathroom. She figured it was her husband until she looked over and saw him lying fast asleep next to her.

The ghost has also locked doors, turned lights on and off, shaken beds while guests are sleeping, extinguished candles, and lit the fireplaces. Apparently William likes to stay busy. The Snow Hill Inn closed in 2008. Since then it appears to have returned to a private residence.

Chapter 26
Around the Eastern Shore

Elsewhere around the Eastern Shore you can encounter a former actor singing in her grave, a twice-buried woman looking for her ring, and a revolutionary making a legendary trip. Then there are the ghosts at two very haunted hotels and possibly even the ghost of Robert E. Lee still hanging out at the Kemp House.

ST. PAUL'S CEMETERY
7579 Sandy Bottom Road, Chestertown, 21629
One of the youngest ghosts happens to haunt one of the oldest Episcopal Church cemeteries in Maryland. But she does it with her own unique style. If you head to St. Paul's Cemetery, head toward the back where the newer graves are. Once there you'll need to place your ear on top of the slab at midnight to hear lyrical singing coming from beneath the ground.

But before you do, you'll need to clear away some of the tokens left on the grave like Mardi Gras beads, cigarettes, playing cards, and at least one empty Vodka bottle. If this seems like odd things to leave on a grave, then you didn't know Tallulah Bankhead. "I want to try everything once," she once said.

Bankhead was an American actor known for her flamboyant personality and her deep, raspy voice. She wasn't known for her singing, so it's strange that she'd take it up now and that her raspy voice would be described as "lyrical." Maybe she regretted never singing on stage or screen, or perhaps she just likes breaking with the norm. It could also be a way to prove it is her. She was named for her grandmother, who in turn was named for a waterfall in Georgia that the Indians called "singing water."

Another ghost haunts a bridge at the edge of the cemetery. Local residents talk of seeing strange lights and shadowy figures on the bridge at night. Others claim to have seen a man sitting under a nearby tree or riding a horse down the road in front of St. Paul's Cemetery.

Many believe it is the ghost of Tench Tilghman. Tilghman was an aide-de-camp to George Washington and carried the message of the British surrender to the Continental Congress. He died when he was forty-one years old, just a few years after the Revolutionary War. He never got a chance to live beyond the war, which may be why he is reliving such a special event.

WHITEMARSH CHURCH
US 50 and Manadier Road, Trappe, 21673

Drive past the Whitemarsh Church Cemetery (known as Hole-in-the-Wall Cemetery on Google Maps) and you may see a woman dressed in old-fashioned clothing walking through the ancient tombstones. Get close enough, and you may hear her moan, "Who's got my golden ring?" You've just met the ghost of Hannah Maynadier, one of the few people who managed to die twice.

An article published on the *Denton Journal* in 1886 tells the story of Mrs. Maynadier: "In 1711, the Rev. Mr. Maynadier was rector, residing at the parsonage on a farm a short distance from [Whitemarsh] church, and a singular story is told of his family. The tradition is that his wife died after a brief illness, and was buried with rather unusual haste. The worthy man, overcome by grief, retired early but was roused from his slumbers shortly before midnight by a knocking at the front door. Imagine his feelings, when, on opening it, there stood his buried wife faint and terrified, but alive and in the flesh. She had been hastily coffined without the removal of a valuable ring, and one of the attendants, aware of the fact, had exhumed the body just after nightfall, for the purposes of robbing it. But the ring clung to the finger and an effort was made to sever the joint; blood flowed, the corpse groaned, moved and recovered consciousness. The would-be robber of the dead fled in terror from the scene, and the lady, thus happily taken from the grave, made her way through the night to the desolate home from which she had been carried a few hours before. She lived to tell the story for many years afterward."

One problem with this story as it was published is Daniel Maynadier didn't marry until January 12, 1720. In 1711, Maynadier had just become the rector of St. Peter's Parish. St. Peter's Parish is also known as Whitemarsh Church. Maynadier remained the rector until his death in 1745. Both he and his wife were buried in a crypt inside the church.

The church was built around 1665 and stood until January 12, 1897, when it was destroyed by a fire. Only two walls of the church remain standing. If that wasn't enough to disturb the Maynandiers, in 1915 his remains were exhumed. Newspaper reports of the event make no mention of Hannah's remains being disturbed. It also only states that remains were exhumed, not that they were stolen.

But disturb a grave, and you're likely to disturb the spirits (or the people living nearby who like to create ghost stories). Legends say Hannah's ghost roams the cemetery in her burial garb and nearby roads moaning, "Who's got my golden ring?" Daniel Maynadier has also been seen in the cemetery.

KEMP HOUSE
412 South Talbot Street, St. Michaels, 21663

A housekeeper for Kemp House, a bed-and-breakfast, was working alone one day. It was early afternoon, the time after the previous night's guests had left but the new guests had not checked in yet, so she was alone. She left the laundry room and was walking toward the office when she saw two men enter the front door. They immediately turned right into the first room.

Not sure who they were, she walked down the hall and stopped outside the door. She could hear the two men talking, but she didn't recognize the voices. Curious about their identity, as no guests were expected this early, she knocked on the door and then opened it. The voices immediately stopped when she opened the door, and no one was inside. Confused, she closed the door and started to turn away when she heard the men talking again. Again, she knocked and then entered but the room was still empty.

Finally, she went to the office and called the front desk, which was located in another building. They confirmed that no guests had checked in or been sent to the Kemp House. The housekeeper was not the first employee to experience the ghosts. People report hearing men's voices, usually on the other side of a door, only to find the room empty upon inspection. Others have seen a blue streak climbing the staircase, followed by hearing a door slamming shut. Things have been moved and rooms rearranged.

Then there is the Blue Room. At night, guests staying in the Blue Room are woken to find the rocking chair moving on its own. Or the end of the bed sinks as if someone was sitting on it. In both cases they report feeling as if someone is staring at them, even though they don't see anyone else in the room. Staff refer to this ghost as "Joseph," after the original owner of the house.

Colonel Joseph Kemp, a hero of the War of 1812, built the house in 1807. A young Robert E. Lee once spent two nights in the house, and some claim his ghost visits every now and then. He is seen standing in a second-story window wearing his Confederate uniform.

UNION HOTEL RESTAURANT & TAVERN
1282 SUSQUEHANNA RIVER ROAD, PORT DEPOSIT, 21904

Doors unlocking and opening, echoing footsteps, objects moving on their own, and a clock that continues to chime without working mechanics are just a few of the things witnessed at Union Hotel Restaurant & Tavern. The building was built around 1790 and has been a tavern, a hotel, and even a brothel at different points in the past. Today it is a restaurant that specializes in colonial-era dining. But keep a watchful eye, as everyone dressed in colonial garb may not be an employee. A lady in a blue gown has been seen by the owner, and some employees have seen a figure known as the "dusty" man. They also report "creepy childlike spirits lurking around the property."

ELK FORGE BED AND BREAKFAST INN
807 ELK MILLS ROAD, ELKTON, 21921

In 1777 the British Redcoats traveled through Elkton on their way toward Philadelphia. On their journey they came across a mill and demanded enormous amounts of flour. The miller obliged, unwillingly, either because he favored revolution or because he knew he wouldn't be paid for his flour. As part of his protest, he put ground glass in with the flour. The British discovered what he did, immediately returned, and hanged him at the site.

The mill has since become the Elk Forge Bed and Breakfast Inn, but the miller remains. His footsteps are often heard walking about the building and his voice is heard. A few people have reported seeing his "melancholic" ghost.

Part 8

BRIDGES AND ROADS

Not all ghosts have the luxury of a nice house or building to haunt. Some are forced to work outside along the bridges and roads of Maryland. While the state seems to have a higher-than-average amount of crybaby bridges, they also offer a well-rounded selection of other types of ghosts, including ghost lights, a spook hill, and even a couple of hitchhiking ghosts.

Chapter 27
Crybaby Bridges

Many people have a fear of bridges, or gephyrophobia. Something about having just a couple of feet between you and falling makes people nervous. And then there are the stories of all the people who have perished on bridges, which often create a few ghost stories.

"Crybaby Bridges," or "Cry Baby Bridges," is a nickname applied to a variety of bridges in Maryland (and across the United States). The short version of the legend is that when you stop your car on the bridge—usually at night—you'll hear a baby cry. The ghostly cry comes from a either a baby or its mother. Although each location puts a spin on things, the stories for these bridges are remarkably similar. A mother and baby are at the bridge one night when the baby (and sometimes the mother) is killed. The death is sometimes accidental, other times murder. In some cases the mother kills the baby and then commits suicide.

Unfortunately, the Internet has spawned a number of crybaby bridges in Maryland to the point that separating the true legends from modern "fakelore" is difficult. Fakelore is manufactured folklore presented as true. Paul Bunyan, Pecos Bill, and Slender Man are all examples of fakelore. While often presented as folklore, their stories were manufactured. One might also refer to them as urban legends.

While the stories behind the tales of crybaby bridges may be manufactured, some of the experiences people have on those bridges might not be. As one drives down a deserted road at night illuminating the darkness, local wilderness stills as a means of protecting itself. Then you stop, turn off the car and lights, and sit in the darkness. Slowly the wildlife relax and resume going about their business . . . which includes making noise.

But surely most people would be able to tell the difference between an animal and a baby.

After all, a number of animals make noises that sound like a crying baby. In Maryland these animals include Siamese cats, raccoons, rabbits, fishers, frogs and toads (especially the Fowler's toad), foxes, coyotes, bobcats, peacocks, and barred owls. Cougars can also make a sound that like that of a crying baby, but they are no longer found in Maryland.

Wouldn't people recognize that the sound is that of an animal and not a baby? Not necessarily. Our minds are designed to make sense of things and categorize them based on our experiences. Most people have heard far more crying babies than Fowler's toads or Siamese cats. So even if they don't know the urban legend, when they hear a sound, they classify it based on what they are most familiar with.

But that doesn't mean all crybaby bridges are faked or simply caused by local animals. A couple have real stories attached to them, which could mean the ghosts associated with them are real.

GOVERNOR'S BRIDGE, BOWIE

If you park your car on or near the bridge, you'll hear a baby crying. Legend says that in the 1930s, a young woman and her baby were murdered here. Other versions of the story say that she wasn't married and, to avoid a scandal, drowned her baby in the river. She then felt so guilty, she jumped in and drowned. Another story says that a family was in a car accident on the bridge. Everyone died except the baby, who died later at the hospital.

Others say that the woman's ghost appears on the side of the bridge. One truck driver ran into the side of the bridge to avoid hitting her. Another couple say that they saw her on their way fishing. As they crossed over the Patuxent River, they were surprised to see a woman, soaked with water, crying hysterically. They stopped to ask the poor woman what was wrong, but the woman vanished before their eyes.

But this bridge isn't just a crybaby bridge. It seems there is no end to the haunted phenomena that occur here. Other times a ghost car creeps up behind you while you are stopped on the bridge. It is described as an old black car. Some say that it will quickly pull up close to you, as if it is going to ram into you, but then it vanishes. Other stories say if you turn to look at it, it vanishes.

Others claim that rocks have pelted their car or hands scratched cars stopped on the road. Impenetrable fog and odd lights have even been reported here. The oddest claim about this bridge is that hanging corpses—including the corpses of children—have been seen here. To get to this bridge, turn on to Governor Bridge Road from Highway 301. Continue on this road about a mile and a half, until you reach the bridge crossing the Patuxent River.

MILL DAM ROAD, MARION STATION

One bridge actually has a true story behind the legend. On July 29, 1875, little Annie Florence Conner was riding from St. Paul's Church toward home with her mother. It started raining, and a clap of thunder or flash of lightning spooked the horses. They reared up and overturned the wagon, which fell into East Creek. Annie was carried downstream by the rushing water. Her body was recovered the following day, according to newspaper accounts of the accident. She was only three years old.

For decades, locals reported hearing a cry when on the bridge. They described it as starting out light, as if in the distance, and then gradually getting louder before abruptly stopping. The bridge, formerly called Mill Dam Bridge, is located on what is now L Q Powel Road. This story was first reported in the 1950s according to local author Woodrow T. Wilson.

LOTTSFORD ROAD, MITCHELLVILLE

On nights when the moon is full, people say you can see a baby going over the bridge and hear his cries on Lottsford Road. He was murdered by one of his parents after they had an argument in the car over the fact that he wouldn't stop crying. Exactly who threw him over the bridge is unclear. The story about the bridge, however, dates back to the 1950s or earlier.

While this story seems to have no historical basis, the road has been nicknamed "The Dumping Grounds," because a number of bodies have turned up there. An exact number is unclear, but according to a 1984 *Washington Post* article, seven murder victims were found on this road between 1974 and 1984. None of them were babies.

The original crybaby bridge and dumping grounds are no longer. In the late 1980s the road was torn out, rerouted, and widened. Housing developments went up, and what was once an isolated road became a modern neighborhood.

SAINT ANDREW'S CHURCH ROAD BRIDGE, HOLLYWOOD

Two stories are connected to Saint Andrew's Church Road Bridge. The first took place during World War II. As if a man isn't already excited to see his wife after an extended absence, this man had even more reason to be happy to return home. His wife had been pregnant before he left, and this was the first time he'd be seeing his son. The woman decided to meet her husband down at the road, so she bundled up the baby. Just before the bridge was a bad turn in the road. The husband struck his wife, killing her instantly. Their child flew out of her arms and into the river. The baby's body was never found. People report hearing a baby crying and seeing a woman on the bridge frantically searching the waters below.

The second story involves a young slave girl who was being raped repeatedly by her owner. One night she struck him in the head with an iron pan, killing him. She gathered her belongings and ran. A posse was formed and hunted her down. They caught her near the bridge and killed her. Now her ghost jumps out in front of cars passing over the bridge, causing minor accidents. Another story claims a slave drowned her baby by throwing it in the river here so it wouldn't be raised into slavery.

Sadly this was a wooden bridge that was removed around 1982 when Route 4 was extended west from Solomons to Leonardtown. The bridge once spanned the western branch of the St. Mary's River.

INDIAN BRIDGE ROAD, GREAT MILLS

Two women and a baby may be heard crying on this bridge. One story is that a man returned home from World War II to find his wife had recently bore a child. Since he had been gone longer than nine months, he knew she had been unfaithful. Infuriated, he ran over the wife and baby and left them to die on the bridge. Another legend says that a slave woman was executed and buried in the marsh after she had murdered her master. The similarity of these stories to those connected to Saint Andrew's Church Road Bridge suggest that this is a case of fakelore. When the other bridge was gone, they moved the stories to this one to continue the legend. The bridge crosses over the St. Mary's River.

PATUXENT ROAD, ODENTON

A woman pushing a stroller appears at midnight on this narrow bridge. Others report hearing a baby cry or seeing a car that vanishes without a trace. Legend says that the mother and baby were struck by a car and killed years ago.

BEAVER DAM ROAD, BELTSVILLE

A lot of sources say there is a crybaby bridge off Beaver Dam Road in Beltsville. No additional details are ever given about it, except that it is near the Henry A. Wallace Beltsville Agricultural Research Center. However, there are no bridges on Beaver Dam Road even remotely near the center. This seems like a case of fakelore.

ADAMS MILL ROAD, WESTMINSTER

Drive over this bridge at night and you can hear babies crying. The most favored legend is that the Ku Klux Klan used the bridge to kill numerous black babies in the 1800s. Others say that a slave owner got his slave pregnant and threw the child over the bridge. There is also the standard girl-afraid-to-tell-her-parents story associated with the bridge. Jesse Glass, a Maryland folklorist and historian, researched the legends associated with this bridge and declared them "fakelore" created by the Internet. The legends seemed to pop up around 1999 and do not have any oral history connected to them. The bridge crosses Little Pipe Creek on Adams Mill Road.

WALNUT TREE ROAD, MILLINGTON

A baby born deformed haunts this bridge. His teenage mother threw him off the bridge after he was born. Besides the typical crying, he also knocks over trees as he throws fits for his lost mother. Car doors lock, windows roll down by themselves, and cars roll backward. These are all said to be things the baby is doing to prevent you from leaving, as he thinks you are his mother. This bridge is also referred to as the Smyrna Crybaby Bridge because it is located between Millington in Maryland and Smyrna in Deleware.

OTHER BRIDGES

Not all haunted bridges in Maryland are crybaby bridges. A few other bridges are haunted by ghosts of people who died on or near the bridge. While the stories are hard to substantiate, it's hard to discount some of them, considering the number of people who have experienced their ghosts.

Jericho Covered Bridge, Kingsville

Travel over the Jericho Covered Bridge at night and you may catch a glimpse of bodies hanging from the rafters. Legend says that slaves caught trying to cross the Mason Dixon Line were hanged from the bridge—sometimes several at a time. Or slaves were hanged there during the Civil War as a political statement. Their bodies can be seen swinging from the rafters at night. But since the bridge wasn't built until 1865, neither story could be true. Lynchings, which were all too common after the war, may be a possibility, but nothing has ever been documented.

Still, quite a few people have claimed to see the bodies. Others say that when they stop at the bridge, they have felt footsteps on the top of their car or the car will start rocking. When they check later, they find hand- and footprints covered in a white film on top of the car. According to *Maryland Ghosts* by Amelia Cotter, the Kelleyano Researchers and Investigators of the Paranormal investigated the bridge. During their investigation they claim to have seen bodies hanging on the bridge and even caught what they interpret as the image of one in a photo. Their car also started shaking on its own.

But the hanging bodies are only one of the stories about the bridge. A girl in a white dress has been seen on the bridge. The stories say that a girl and her father were crossing the bridge at night when a lantern turned over. The girl burned to death. Her face was burned into the bottom of the bridge and could be viewed there until renovations covered it up. Her ghost is said to haunt here. A more modern version of this story says that a kerosene lamp overturned in the back of a truck, and that's how the girl died. Her screams have also been heard coming from the bridge.

Then there is the standard bridge story that says a woman threw her baby off the bridge. Not only do people say they can hear the baby crying, but that the woman is seen in the area around the bridge. She is described as wearing a 1800s-style dress and carrying a basket. Jericho Covered Bridge crosses Little Gunpowder Falls on Jericho Road.

HEARTBEAT BRIDGE, ELLICOTT CITY

Late at night, if you pause your car on "Heartbeat Bridge" and listen, you will hear—and possibly feel—a heart beating. Two versions of the legend exist to explain the phenomenon. The first is that a husband who lived near the bridge went insane and murdered his wife. He cut out her heart and threw it off the bridge. The second is that a wealthy white girl fell in love with a slave. Knowing they couldn't be together, they jumped off the bridge together. You only hear one heart beating, because their two hearts now beat as one.

The sources say that the bridge is "off Bonnie Branch Road." Since there are no real bridges on Bonnie Branch Road, the most likely location of the bridge is the one on Ilchester Road over the Patapsco River—especially since one poster about the bridge reported that an "old man with dogs and an axe" lived near the bridge and would chase people off. Ilchester Road is very close to Saint Mary's Ruins (see St. Mary's College in chapter 10.)

UTICA MILLS COVERED BRIDGE, THURMONT

Late one foggy night a couple was traveling home. As the man drove over the Utica Mills Covered Bridge, a young boy appeared in front of his car. He immediately slammed on the breaks, but it was too late. The car didn't stop in time to prevent hitting the boy. The man jumped out of his car and dropped down to look under the car, but nothing was there. He looked up. The boy was standing a few feet behind the rear of his car. The boy stared blankly at the man, his hair and clothes dripping water. The man started to speak, but the boy disappeared.

Locals say that the boy drowned in the creek years ago when the area underneath was used as a swimming hole. Children stopped going there after he drowned, fearing they would suffer the same fate. Now his ghost haunts the bridge. People report seeing a glowing apparition climbing out of Fishing Creek or hear cries coming from the water. The bridge crosses Fishing Creek on Utica Road.

RODDY COVERED BRIDGE, THURMONT

The ghosts of Confederate soldiers have been seen around the Roddy Covered Bridge. The legends differ on how they ended up haunting the bridge. Some say they were raiding farms around the area and spent the night at the bridge. Some men confronted them, a small conflict ensued, and several soldiers died. While there are records of Confederate soldiers moving through the area, no specifics on any one dying near the bridge exist. The Roddy Covered Bridge crosses Owens Creek over Roddy Road.

Chapter 28

Haunted Roads

Driving along a darkened road, alone, can make a person on edge, anxious. But that anxiety increases when you know that you may not be as alone as you should be. It might be a ghostly hitchhiker, a phantom car, or a former murder victim.

SPOOK HILL, BURKITTSVILLE

On a small back road between Boonsboro and Burkittsville, if you place your car in neutral, ghosts will push your car uphill. The ghosts are those of Civil War soldiers who were pushing a cannon uphill when they were killed. Now, like the Greek Sisyphus, they are continually pushing things up this hill. In fact, if you place flour on the back of your car, you will see their handprints where they touched the car. One person who experienced the phenomenon sat on the back of his car and said he could feel hands pushing him.

While the story sounds great, this isn't a paranormal phenomenon but a simple optical illusion. While the spot appears to be an incline, it isn't. The spot occurs when the horizon is hidden or barely visible and usually perpendicular objects, like trees, lean. The two things mess with our ability to judge the slope of a surface. An easy way to prove that the issue is an illusion is to pour water on the spot and see which way it flows.

But what causes the handprints? The flour is usually put on the back of the car, on the trunk, where people usually place their hands to close it. The flour simply illuminates the handprints that are already there. To get to the hill, turn on Gapland Road toward Gathland State Park. The spot is between the large red barn on the left and Mountain Church Road.

OLD RAILROAD ROAD, HEBRON

An eerie "dull yellow" or "pinkish orange" light floats along Old Railroad Road south of Route 54. The light gained a lot of publicity in 1952 after two state troopers reported seeing it twenty feet from their car. They attempted to catch up with it, but it always stayed out of reach. Scientists claimed it was just swamp gas, but the light behaved differently. Others claimed it was the ghost of someone who died in the area (train engineer, Patty Cannon, train/car accident victim). Over the years, hundreds of people traveled out to the road and reported seeing the light. Sightings of the light diminished after the road was paved in 1974.

BLACK ROCK ROAD, GERMANTOWN

According to the myth, two teenage girls died on this road after they crashed into "a small lake close to an old water house." At night, if you turn off your car lights and honk your horn, the spirits of the girls will rise from the lake and tap on your car door. Some reports say that you should "drive on the road with no car lights to see their ghostly images." (Author's note: I think that should be "join" them as it would be extremely stupid to drive down a two lane road at night without lights.) Others report that bright headlights are seen but disappear without a trace of a car.

According to Google Maps there is no "lake" on this road. There are a couple of nearby ponds, but you'd have to work hard to crash into them. But more important, all the stories found about this road are nearly word-for-word identical, suggesting it's just another Internet legend that spread. One interesting thing though: This road does pass over Seneca Creek near where "Coffin Rock" is located, made famous in the fictional *The Blair Witch Project*. (It may or may not have been called Coffin Rock before the movie.) This area may also be where Heather parks her car at the start of the hike.

BOTTOM ROAD, FALSTON

A little girl in a white dress holding a teddy bear is seen standing along Bottom Road. When concerned motorists stop, they notice that her face is streaked with tears and her dress is torn and blood stained. As they approach her, she vanishes. Legend says she was raped and murdered in the woods. There are no specifics on where her ghost can be found, except it is at the "narrow part past the residential area and fields." Nothing about this story has been substantiated.

KEENERS ROAD, MIDDLE RIVER

It's just a little side road off Carroll Island Road, but locals call it "Ghost Road." If you drive down this road, past the housing developments to where it is lined with trees and there are railroad tracks, strange things will start happen. Car headlights and radios turn off. Sometimes your car engine dies. Something starts pounding on the outside of the vehicle. On some nights, on the right-hand side of the road, a tombstone can be seen in the woods. The tombstone has a bluish tinge to it, and there is a figure floating beside it. There used to be a large, old, abandoned house on the road that was also haunted, but no sign of it can be found today.

NOTCHCLIFF ROAD, GLEN ARM

According to online postings about Notchcliff Road, if you drive on the road at 11:30 at night, "double yellow lines slowly disappear and around the next turn, off in the distance you can see headlights and a mangled car. As you drive closer it slowly disappears and there is a tree with red 'paint,' busted up from the car." This may have once been true, but today there are no yellow lines on Notchcliff Road. It is a very narrow road with many sharp curves. Numerous accidents have occurred on this road as a result. Anyone hunting ghosts should be very careful.

MILLER'S CHURCH ROAD, HAGERSTOWN

According to legends, in the 1930s, a Catholic church known as "Miller's Church" was taken over by devil worshippers who sacrificed young girls. The church burned down and all that was left was a big oak. One night a couple went parking there. But when they decided to leave, the car wouldn't start. The boy went for help. When he returned, the girl was hanging from the oak tree. Her ghost can still be seen hanging from the tree. Also, a phantom hearse comes and chases people away from this spot.

There was a Miller's Church, but it was a Mennonite church and still stands at 20866 Miller's Church Road. What most people mistake as being the burnt-down "Miller's Church" was actually Jacob's Lutheran Church. The church and cemetery were all but abandoned after the church closed in the early 1970s. This church eventually burned down sometime in the 1970s or 1980s. In 2000, locals made a concerted effort to clean up the overgrown cemetery. It was likely the property's abandonment and neglect that fueled the tall tales. Jacob's Church is located north of the Mennonite church near a sharp turn in the road.

On a side note, the stories about being chased by a hearse could be true. Some say a neighbor got tired of all the vandalism and bought a hearse. He then used it to chase away curious teenagers.

OTHER ROADS

Daisy Lane in Bowie is believed to be haunted by a girl who was abducted and murdered in 1995. Her body was found on Daisy Lane, and her murder is still unsolved.

A large black dog dragging a chain haunts **Cherryfield Road** in Drayden.

On **Honeysuckle Road** in Crownsville, the ghosts of two girls and an elderly man roam. They were killed by a psycho many years ago.

The underpass that runs under US 340 on **Elmer Road**, just off Elmer Derr Road, is haunted by the ghost of a motorcyclist who was killed there years ago.

If you stop your car on **Route 32** in Crownsville at 2:30 a.m., a car's headlights will suddenly appear behind you. A woman will get out of the car and ask you if everything is all right. As she returns to her car, she and the car disappear.

Route 450 between Crofton and Bowie has Maryland's first version of the hitchhiking ghost. She is dressed in a 1920s flapper dress. People who stop to offer her a ride report that she shakes her head and vanishes.

Another version of the hitchhiking ghost wanders **Route 40** wearing a low-cut, blue sequin cocktail dress. She lets people give her a ride home, but when she keeps your coat, you'll have to go to her gravesite to retrieve it.

Also on **Route 40** is "Death Curve," located where the road curves sharply near Antietam Creek. This spot has a higher than average number of accidents, and some claim that the victims have come back to haunt it. One is a headless man who is seen walking along the side of the road.

Appendix A
Other Locations

A few locations in Maryland are reported to be haunted, but not much is known about the hauntings. These stories are included here. The locations are arranged by region and include addresses.

BALTIMORE

BALTIMORE THEATRE PROJECT

At least a couple times a year, people report hearing or seeing someone playing the piano here. Those who have heard him play, always remark on how wonderful the music is. No one knows who he is, but the music he plays seems like it is from the 1920s. The Theatre Project is located on 45 West Preston Street in Baltimore.

GARRETT-JACOBS MANSION

Robert Garrett, president of the B & O Railroad, built the mansion in 1884. After his death, his wife married Henry Barton Jacobs, giving the mansion its second name. The Engineer's Club took over the building in 1961. Housekeepers report seeing objects moving on their own in the basement. The comptroller frequently saw a shadowy figure pass her in the second-floor hallway. A heavy sculpture moved back to its original position after it was relocated. Faucets and showers turn on by themselves. Peter Weston, the former food and beverage director, reported seeing a handyman sitting in the lobby one day. The odd thing was the handyman had resigned a month earlier right before he passed away. It wasn't until after he greeted the man that he realized his error. When Weston turned around, the handyman had vanished. The Engineer's Club is located at 11 West Mount Vernon Place in Baltimore.

Loyola College

McAuley Hall is a residence hall with some ghostly residents. People have seen objects fall off shelves, even though they weren't even close to the edge. Doors close on their own, sometimes slamming shut. One student even saw a young man in her room that vanished when she approached. Loyola College is located at 4501 North Charles Street in Baltimore.

Phantom of O'Donnell Heights

In July 1951, residents of this neighborhood reported seeing a strange black-capped creature. Over two hundred people claimed to have seen him. People heard him walking on their roofs. One girl said he tried to entice her from under a car. Every break-in and odd occurrence in the neighborhood was blamed on the phantom. One man claimed he chased the phantom, which disappeared into a nearby cemetery and vanished under a sarcophagus. A vigilante team was formed to try and capture him, but they never caught him. He eventually vanished and was never seen again.

Ryleigh's Oysters

Almost every employee has an experience while working here. One pushed in a chair only to find it pushed out and turned around when she returned. Noises including loud thuds are heard coming from the second floor when no one is up there. Objects are moved around. Lights dim and the stereo has turned itself on. One woman was walking down the stairs when she tripped. A strange force stopped her from falling and deposited her on the bottom stairs. The restaurant is located at 36 East Cross Street in Baltimore.

VERDE

Back when it was a restaurant known as Birches, the owners claimed it was haunted. The phones would light up at 12:15 a.m. If you picked it up, you got nothing but a dial tone. The phone company couldn't explain it. On the second floor, employees have heard their name called. Doors open and shut on their own. The water has turned on by itself. Footsteps have also been heard. No word if the new owners have similar experiences. Verde is located at 641 South Montford Avenue in Baltimore.

ANNAPOLIS

EDEN'S GHOSTLY PROCESSION

Sir Robert Eden was the last English governor. He fled to England at the start of the Revolutionary War and didn't return to Maryland until 1784. He was given a mixed reception when he returned, because he was known to have been friendly with both sides. Upon his death, friends were concerned that his body might become a target of vengeful patriots. So, in the middle of the night, Eden's coffin was carried down Shipwright Street to a boat at Spa Creek. It was then taken to St. Margaret's Churchyard for burial. Witnesses have reported seeing a group of ghostly slaves with lanterns carrying a coffin down Shipwright Street on dark, foggy nights.

GOVERNOR CALVERT HOUSE

The former home of Governor Calvert is said to be haunted by several ghosts including that of a woman who committed suicide in the 1940s and an eighteenth-century gentleman. In the 1980s, a paranormal group investigated the building and reported that one of the ghosts was named Dominic. Dominic liked haunting the building since it had become an inn because it gave him an opportunity to watch women take their clothes off. Calvert House is located on 58 State Circle in Annapolis.

HAMMOND-HARWOOD HOUSE

According to legend, a young man was building the Hammond-Harwood house for his beloved. However, she grew impatient and accused him of spending more time on the house than with her and broke off the engagement. The young man forever remained a bachelor. On moonlit nights the lady's ghost returns to the house she scorned and searches for her lost love. This is one story where the history seems to fit with the legend. The house was built by Matthias Hammond in 1774. However, it does not seem he ever lived in the house. He moved to his family's country estate in 1776. He never married and died in 1786. The house is located on 19 Maryland Avenue in Annapolis.

PACA HOUSE AND GARDEN

William Paca was a member of the Continental Congress and one of Maryland's four signers of the Declaration of Independence. He constructed his house in 1765. It underwent a complete renovation in the 1970s that seemed to restore Paca's spirit. Watchmen assigned during the renovation frequently saw a ghost dressed in colonial attire. The sightings were so frequent that some refused to continue working there. Paca House is located on 186 Prince George Street in Annapolis.

CENTRAL

CURRIER HOUSE

An eight-year-old girl haunts one of the rooms of this bed-and-breakfast. She moves objects around, such as shaking the hangers if you try to talk to her. She calls herself "G. Z." No one has been able to identify her, possibly because she was in the house when it was part of the Underground Railroad. The house is located at 800 Market Street in Havre De Grace.

GRACE ROCKY HILL LUTHERAN CHURCH CEMETERY

A tombstone bleeds in this Woodsboro cemetery. A woman warned her husband that if he remarried and his new wife was cruel to her children, her tombstone would bleed. Sure enough, the new wife abused the children and the tombstone started bleeding. The woman's grave is located in the left-hand corner of the cemetery, three rows back in the middle of the row. The name is no longer legible, but a plaque marks the grave. It is located at 10825 Coppermine Road in Woodsboro.

THE LAWN

The Lawn is a nineteenth-century house that remained in the Dobbin family until 1951. Shortly after it changed hands, poltergeist activity began. Doors have locked and unlocked themselves, and people report hearing scratching sounds. Objects also move about. The key to the grandfather clock would disappear and then reappear later. A head of lettuce shot straight up in front of several witnesses. Toilet paper disappeared. The residents replaced it, only to have it disappear again. Flowers were pulled out from window boxes by their roots. A medicine cabinet was found locked, and no one could open it. Months later, the owner found it open. The Lawn is located at 6036 Old Lawyers Hill Road in Elkridge.

OLD MEDIX SCHOOL

Years ago, a hotel stood at 700 York Road in Towson. One day, a man killed himself after his fiancée refused to marry him. Eventually, the hotel closed and a school opened in the building. The room the man died in was transformed into a teachers' lounge. In the lounge, filing cabinets would open and doorknobs turned. He didn't stay in his room. People also heard footsteps, and the elevator often moved on its own. The original building has since been torn down.

PERRYMAN MANSION

Mysterious voices and terrible odors are experienced at this now-crumbling manor house. Orbs and odd lights are found in photographs taken here. Strange green lights have also been seen moving about the house. An abnormal amount of animal bones are said to be found here. The house was purchased years ago by Baltimore Gas and Electric Company and simply left to decay. It is located on the Perryman peninsula in Harford County.

TODD'S INHERITANCE

The farm dates back to the War of 1812, as it was rebuilt after the British burned it down after failing to capture Fort

McHenry. There are three stories connected with this house, all of them take place at night. A woman with a candle is seen waiting in the attic window for her soldier who never returned home. If an intruder breaks into the house, lights come on even though the house has no electricity. Finally, if you look toward the family cemetery, you can see slaves hanging from the trees. The house is located at 9000 North Point Road in Edgemere.

YELLOW TURTLE INN
An older woman in white wanders the second- and third-floor hallways of this bed-and-breakfast. She may be wearing a white dress or robe. Lights also flicker on the third floor. Former residents also reported hearing the sound of marbles rolling down the hallway in the middle of the night. The property is said to contain an unmarked cemetery, and the ghosts are trying to find other ways to commemorate their passing. It used to be known as the Windsor Castle Inn and is located at 111 Springdale Avenue in New Windsor.

CAPITAL

BEATTY-CRAMER HOUSE
Members of the Betty and Cramer families are said to roam the grounds of this house. The house combined the Beatty House, built in 1732, and the Cramer House, built in 1855. The Beatty-Cramer House is located at 9010 Liberty Road in Frederick.

CATOCTIN FURNACE

Catoctin Furnace is haunted by a Union solder. He was burned alive after being caught by the Confederates. His ghost has been seen pointing his rifle at tourists. The furnace is now part of Cunningham Falls State Park in Thurmont.

CLARA BARTON HOUSE

Clara Barton is said to be haunting her former home. She spent the last fifteen years of her life and eventually passed away here at the age of ninety. People report seeing an old woman walking the halls or hearing her voice. Residents frequently see her peering out from a window or through the front door. The house is located at 5801 Oxford Road in Glen Echo.

OXON HILL CEMETERY

Two little girls have been seen wandering in the cemetery late at night. They vanish when approached. A gravestone in the cemetery contains the name of two girls who died in the same month and year. The cemetery is located behind the post office on Oxon Hill Road in Oxon Hill-Glassmanor.

PAINT BRANCH HOME

People have heard slaves singing at all times of the day and night here. Residents of the assisted-living center reported seeing a figure with tattered clothing at the end of their beds, looking at them angrily. The center was closed and put up for sale in 2011. The for sale ad read: "Owner selling property 'AS IS' condition. Seller makes no representation or warranties as to the property condition . . . ENTER AT YOUR OWN RISK!" It is located at 3120 Powder Mill Road, Adelphi.

St. Andrew's Episcopal School

A dark figure has been seen walking through the school. People also hear footsteps and feel cold spots in the school. A farmhouse built by Thomas Claggett in the 1800s is now part of this school. The ghost may be a former resident or Thomas himself. The school used to be known as Harker Preparatory School and is located at 8804 Postoak Road in Potomac.

SOUTHERN

Northern Middle and High School

The northwest section of the high school is believed to have been built over a slave graveyard. The slaves worked at the Old Ward House on Flint Hill Road. Angered over the slight, the slaves haunt the classrooms by flinging posters and other objects. One October, students felt a warm breeze that closed the hallway door and opened the outside door. White material has fallen from the ceiling, although no source for it was found. In one of the art rooms, a ceramic pot shot up in the air and then landed on the floor unbroken. Teachers and custodians have heard voices after the school was closed. One heard chairs being dragged across the stage, although no one was in the room at the time. Lights turn on and off mysteriously. Some have reported hearing chains being dragged and moaning. The schools are located at 2950-2954 Chaneyville Road in Owings.

Solomon's Island

A lighthouse is located at 14630 Solomons Island Road in Solomon. When this was the Bowen's Inn, an employee, Robert, was carrying boxes to the third floor when he saw a ghostly woman standing on the top of the stair landing. He said she was very tall with an old-fashioned black dress with a white lace collar. He immediately started backing down the stairs as he watched her turn and walk down the hall. He never returned to the third floor.

When the building at 14560 Solomons Island Road was the Gray Fox Inn, a small ghostly poodle was seen. It belonged to the original owner who built the home in 1913. The dog doesn't always fully materialize. Sometimes only his tail is seen wagging on the floor. The building now houses several retail stores.

Carmen's Gallery is located at 14550 Solomons Island Road. Strange noises are often heard in the building, which are believed to be the ghost of a former resident. People say a man staying there in the 1940s fell off the pier and drowned. The new owner found his suitcase still packed in the attic.

WESTERN

ANTIETAM CREEK

Residents of Funktown claim that on September 12 the ghost of a young Indian maiden paddles her canoe up Antietam Creek. She was a young Catawa who fell in love with a boy from Delaware. The two met at the creek. One day he didn't show up, and she later learned he had died in an accident. In distress, she drowned herself in the creek. On the anniversary of her death, her spirit searches for her lost love.

The Castle

The previous owner of this stone house, Andrew Ramsay, is said to haunt it. Today it is a bed-and-breakfast. It is located at 15925 Mount Savage Road in Mount Savage.

Chaney House

A figure of a nurse wearing a nineteenth-century nurses uniform has been seen roaming the upstairs of the Chaney House. During the Civil War, the house served as the main hospital during the Battle of Funkstown on July 10, 1863. This battle was part of the Gettysburg Campaign. People have also heard someone playing the piano late at night. Apparently, a customer purchased an antique table from the shop, and all the haunting stopped, at least at Chaney House. The customer reported the nurse had come home with her. Chaney House is located at 1 South High Street in Funkstown.

Fort Frederick

A woman in white haunts Fort Frederick. Her husband died while at the fort. Now she is spending eternity looking for him. Those interested in finding her should consider the annual ghost walk put on by Fort Frederick every October. The fort is located at 11100 Fort Frederick Road in Big Pool.

Frostburg State University

One of the fraternity houses here claims to be haunted by the ghost of a sorority girl. The young woman was raped and killed while trying to hitchhike home after the spring semester in 1988. Her boyfriend lived in the house, and other brothers always complained that she left her hair dryer plugged in in the upstairs bathroom. After her death, two brothers heard a hair dryer running in that bathroom.

When they investigated, the room was very steamy and the words "Hitch A Ride" were written on the mirror. No hair dryer was ever found.

Lions Community Park
Rumor says this park was built over an Indian burial ground. Unexplained drumming is heard in this area. Dogs also act crazy when brought to the park. Some even claim to have seen ghosts here. The park is located at 238 Shaw Street in Frostburg.

The Old Depot
People report hearing the sound of a steam train whistle when no trains are running. Even "stranger sounds" are heard coming from a tunnel that runs under Main Street, although no one explains what that means. It is located at 13 Canal Street in Cumberland.

Old Leiter House
Residents report hearing odd sounds from the basement and strange, moving vibrations. They believe they are the ghosts of the Van Leiter family. A photograph also caught a ghostly man sitting in the driveway in an antique car. The Leiter House is a private residence on Main Street in Leitersburg.

Tipuhato House
The former owner of this house refused to leave after she passed away. Katherine Taylor built the house as a summer home in 1902. When new owners purchased it in 1985, they reported hearing footsteps, including the sound of someone pacing in the bedroom, and that objects were moved around. They also had the feeling of being watched. It is a private home located on Raven Rock Road in Cascade.

WASHINGTON MONUMENT

The first monument to George Washington was built on South Mountain in Boonsboro. Legend says during the Civil War a soldier stopped at a farm to get a drink and fell in love with the farmer's daughter. Fearing for his life, the young woman begged him to run away from the war and hide. He agreed. Together, the young couple went to the caves where a rockslide trapped them. At night you can hear them crying for help. The monument is located inside Washington Monument State Park located at 6620 Zittlestown Road in Middletown.

WILLIAMSPORT TOWN HALL

Williamsport Town Hall is also haunted by an employee, but this time his daughter has some doubts. Warren "Bus" Seymour was the Williamsport town clerk for forty-two years, until he was elected mayor. He died in 1985 while in office. People claim to hear him typing on his typewriter. He is also heard walking in the hallways and jingling his keys, according to his daughter, Elissa Slayman, in a *Herald-Mail* article published in 2011. Seymour may be alone. A little girl has been seen in the conference room and apparently likes to play with flashlights. The town hall is located at 2 North Conococheague Street in Williamsport.

EASTERN SHORE

THE CANNONBALL HOUSE

What happens when a cannonball bounces off your chimney, goes through a second-story window, and rolls down your steps during the War of 1812? Your house gets named the Cannonball House! The ghosts here have nothing to do with that event, although no one is sure where they came from. People hear footsteps walking through the house and on the stairs. The house is located at 200 Mulberry Street in St. Michaels.

Cecil County Detention Center
If you knowingly build over or even near an Indian grave-yard, you're doomed to be haunted. When the center opened in 1984, it had a collection of arrowheads and pottery that was unearthed by archaeologists before construction began. It also had disembodied footsteps and lights that turned on and off by themselves. People heard a howling sound that moved through the hallway. One inmate was pinned down by the figure of an Indian in a feathered headdress and war paint. He refused to sleep in a cell alone after that. The detention center is located at 500 Landing Lane in Elkton.

Furnace Town
A small village was created here in 1832 by the Maryland Iron Company when it employed hundreds of people to operate its iron mines built here. The people built their homes around it. Around one hundred homes plus a general store, church, school, and a few other buildings were built here. The furnaces eventually closed and the workers moved on, all except Samson Hat. He refused to leave and stayed in the town and hoped to be buried there. He lived there until he was 106 years old and the county forced him to move to an almshouse, where he died the following year. He wasn't buried in Furnace Town, which is why people believe his ghost haunts here. People have seen a tall black man walking through the village who disappears. Furnace

Town has been restored and is now open to the public. It is located five miles north of Snow Hill on Old Furnace Road off Route 12.

INN AT MITCHELL HOUSE

Mitchell House was built in the early 1800s. One of the ghosts likes to rock in the rocking chair in Room 4. Those who have sat in the chair claim to feel something (or someone) touching their legs. The owner's cat refuses to enter the room, while the dog is often found playing in the room with someone only he can see. Weird sounds are heard throughout the house. The basement has an eerie feeling to it. It used to house slaves. During a paranormal investigation, visitors heard heavy objects being moved and found items blocking their path that hadn't been there moments before. Cold spots also are experienced in the basement. The inn is located at 8796 Maryland Parkway in Chestertown.

KENT MANOR INN

When this former home was being turned into an inn, the new owners were asked if they had seen the previous owner, Alexander Thompson. Previous as in he owned the house in the 1800s. His ghost has been seen riding a white horse up the drive to the house. He's just one of the ghosts in the house. Room 209 is the most haunted room. Lights turn off and on and the television turns itself off. People say they feel as if someone is watching them. One guest heard knocking all night long. An employee saw a male ghost sitting on the bed in Room 303 and ran screaming out of the building. All the unrented rooms are locked each night. The next morning, they are found unlocked and their doors open. The inn is located at 500 Kent Manor Drive in Stevensville.

SALISBURY UNIVERSITY

Halloway Hall is the oldest building on campus with its own bell tower. Legend says the bell tower is haunted by a student who committed suicide there. The university is located at 1101 Camden Avenue in Salisbury.

TEACKLE MANSION

Built in 1802, this house went through a number of residents before becoming a museum. Some of the residents have decided not to leave. A tenant saw the figure of a woman in his room. He left the building and never returned. The alarm system frequently goes off in the middle of the night without cause. People also experience cold spots through the house. During an investigation, paranormal investigators had batteries in a two-way radio, digital camera, and video camera all die in the same spot at the same time. The mansion is located at 11736 Mansion Street in Princess Anne.

WHITE HOUSE FARM

As the story goes, one night a young indentured servant, Mary Stewart, planned on eloping with her lover. As she was leaving to meet him, she fell from her horse and died instantly. The rock where she hit her head still has the blood stains. People have tried painting over it, but the stains show through. Mary still haunts White House Farm, where she lived before her death. Footsteps are heard pacing back and forth on the second floor and in the dining room. Doors open and close by themselves. The dogs bark at nothing. People feel as if they are being watched. A woman awoke to see a woman wearing a blue nightgown walking through her room. The woman is believed to be the ghost of Mary Perkins, who inherited the house from her father. Some say the ghost of George Washington, who visited but never lived here, also haunts the place. White House Farm is a private residence at 11154 Augustine Herman Highway in Chestertown.

Appendix B
Selected Sources

BOOKS

Barefoot, Daniel W. *Spirits of '76: Ghost Stories of the American Revolution*. Winston-Salem, NC: John F. Blair, Publisher, 2009.

Belanger, Jeff. *Encyclopedia of Haunted Places Ghostly Locales from around the World*. Rev. ed. Franklin Lakes, NJ: New Page Books, 2009.

Burgoyne, Mindie. *Haunted Eastern Shore: Ghostly Tales from East of the Chesapeake*. Charleston, SC: Haunted America, 2009.

Burgoyne, Mindie. *Haunted Ocean City & Berlin*. History Press, 2014.

Cohen, Daniel. *Civil War Ghosts*. New York: Scholastic, 1999.

Coleman, Christopher Kiernan. *Ghosts and Haunts of the Civil War: Authentic Accounts of the Strange and Unexplained*. Nashville, TN: Rutledge Hill Press, 1999.

Cotter, Amelia. *Maryland Ghosts: Paranormal Encounters in the Free State*. Rockford, IL: Black Oak Media, 2012.

Coulombe, Charles A. *Haunted Places in America*. Guilford, CT: Lyons Press, 2004.

Crain, Mary Beth. *Haunted U.S. Battlefields: Ghosts, Hauntings, and Eerie Events from America's Fields of Honor.* Guilford, CT: Globe Pequot Press, 2008.

Cutler, Robin R. *A Soul on Trial: A Marine Corps Mystery at the Turn of the Twentieth Century.* Lanham, MD: Rowman & Littlefield, 2007.

Diehl, Daniel, and Mark Donnelly. *Haunted Houses: Guide to Spooky, Creepy, and Strange Places across the USA.* Mechanicsburg, PA: Stackpole Books, 2010.

Fair, Susan. *Mysteries and Lore of Western Maryland: Snallygasters, Dogmen, and Other Mountain Tales.* Charleston, SC: History Press, 2013.

Gallagher, Trish. *Ghosts & Haunted Houses of Maryland.* Centreville, MD: Tidewater Publishers, 1988.

Glass, Jesse. *Ghosts and Legends of Carroll County, Maryland.* Westminster, MD: Carroll County Public Library, 1982.

Graham, Stacey. *Haunted Stuff: Demonic Dolls, Screaming Skulls and Other Creepy Collectibles.* Woodbury, MN: Llewellyn, 2014.

Harding, John. *Sailing's Strangest Moments.* London: Robson, 2004.

Lake, Matthew, and Mark Sceurman. *Weird Maryland: Your Travel Guide to Maryland's Local Legends and Best Kept Secrets.* New York: Sterling Pub., 2006.

Lottes, Karen Yaffe, and Dorothy Pugh. *In Search of Maryland Ghosts: Montgomery County.* Arglen, PA: Schiffer, 2012.

Nesbitt, Mark. *Civil War Ghost Trails: Stories from America's Most Haunted Battlefields.* Mechanicsburg, PA: Stackpole, 2012.

Newman, Rich. *The Ghost Hunter's Field Guide: Over 1000 Haunted Places You Can Experience.* Woodbury, MN: Llewellyn Publications, 2011.

Norman, Michael, and Beth Scott. *Historic Haunted America.* New York: TOR, 1995.

Okonowicz, Ed. *Annapolis Ghosts: History, Mystery, Legends and Lore.* Elkton, MD: Myst and Lace Pub., 2007.

———. *Baltimore Ghosts: History, Mystery, Legends and Lore.* Elkton, MD: Myst and Lace Pub., 2004.

———. *Haunted Maryland Ghosts and Strange Phenomena of the Old Line State.* Mechanicsburg, PA: Stackpole Books, 2007.

Riccio, Dolores, and Joan Bingham. *Haunted Houses USA.* New York: Pocket Books, 1989.

Ricksecker, Mike. *Ghosts of Maryland.* Arglen, PA: Schiffer, 2010.

Rowall, Melissa, and Any Lynwander. *Baltimore's Harbor Haunts.* Arglen, PA: Schiffer, 2005.

Varhola, Michael O., and Michael H. Varhola. *Ghosthunting Maryland.* Cincinnati, OH: Clerisy Press, 2009.

Williams, David. *A People's History of the Civil War: Struggles for the Meaning of Freedom.* New York: New Press, 2005.

ARTICLES

Barkley, Kristin Harty. "Paranormal Investigator Believes Cumberland Restaurant Haunted." *Cumberland Times-News.* October 29, 2010. Accessed August 14, 2015. www.times-news.com/news/local_news/paranormal -investigator-believes-cumberland-restaurant-haunted/ article_6a5499fb-4ad7-5c65-920d-95f94a07417a.html.

Brick, Krista. "Ghosttracker Has Plenty of Weird Tales." *Frederick News-Post.* October 27, 2003. Accessed August 9, 2015.

Carroll County Public Library, Staff. "Ghost Walk of Carrol County." Accessed August 24, 2015. www.westgov.com/ DocumentCenter/View/183

"Fells Point Serves Up More than Just Spirits." ABC2News .com. October 31, 2012. Accessed July 28, 2015.

Goessl, Leigh. "Civil War Ghosts: Is Burnside Bridge at Antietam Haunted? (Includes First-hand Account)." Digital Journal. January 26, 2013. Accessed August 12, 2015. www.digitaljournal.com/article/342148.

Guynn, Susan. "Ghosts & Gobblins of a Local Kind." *Frederick News-Post*. October 26, 2009. Accessed September 12, 2015. www.fredericknewspost.com/archive/ghosts -gobblins-of-a-local-kind/article_4fb4ae39-84f0-5736 -a4c5-6632bf6f7ea9.html.

Holmes, Tamara E. "Haunted Haunts" Gazette.net. October 27, 2004. Accessed August 29, 2015. ww2.gazette .net/gazette_archive/2004/200444/entertainment/ coverstory/242675-1.html.

Opsasnick, Mark. "Crybaby Bridge." *Strange* magazine. Accessed September 10, 2015. www.strangemag.com/ strangemag/strange21/crybabybridge21.html.

Roche, Dylan. "A Halloween Haunting: The Ghosts of Pasadena." *Pasadena Voice*. October 19, 2011. Accessed July 25, 2015. www.pasadenavoice.com/community/ halloween-haunting-ghosts-pasadena.

Snow, Justin. "Spooky Baltimore." *Baltimore* magazine. October 2011. Accessed July 22, 2015. www.baltimore magazine.net/2011/9/spooky-baltimore.

Widener, Christina. "Mystery Lives Here: Local Ghost Stories." *Hagerstown Magazine—The Best of Life in Washington County & Beyond*. September 1, 2006. Accessed September 12, 2015.

WEBSITES

American Hauntings: Ghostly Books, Tours, Events & Information: www.prairieghosts.com

Ghost Stories: paranormalstories.blogspot.com

Haunted Houses.com: www.hauntedhouses.com

The Haunted Internet: www.thehauntedinternet.com

Haunted Places.org: www.hauntedplaces.org

Maryland Historical Trust Index of Historical Places: mdihp.net/index.cfm

Seeks Ghosts: hseeksghosts.blogspot.com

StrangeUSA.com: www.strangeusa.com

Southern Spirit Guide: southernspiritguide.blogspot.com

Unexplainable.net: www.unexplainable.net

Who Cares What I Think?: www.marylandwriter.net

ABOUT THE AUTHOR

Darcy Oordt grew up in a ghostly desert: There is not one known haunted house in her hometown of Blue Earth, Minnesota. It wasn't until she moved to Tennessee that she experienced her first ghost while working as a guide for a "ghost" tour. Her first book, *Finding Success After Failure: Inspirational Stories of Famous People Who Persevered and Won Out,* tells about the early failures of famous people and how they overcame them. In her free time, Darcy enjoys swimming with sharks, flipping houses, and exploring museums in exotic locations . . . if by "enjoy" you mean watching on television. When she is not writing, you will usually find her spending time with her foster cats (which allow her to be the crazy cat lady writer she knows she is without actually owning a dozen cats). Darcy also enjoys making jewelry and other crafts, fussing with one of her freshwater aquariums, and advocating for animals. She is also the author of *Haunted Philadelphia.*